The Spiritual Teachings of

SENECA

Also by Mark Forstater

THE SPIRITUAL TEACHINGS OF
MARCUS AURELIUS
THE SPIRITUAL TEACHINGS OF THE TAO

Visit the *Spiritual Teachings* website at
www.spiritualteachings.info

The Spiritual Teachings of
SENECA

Mark Forstater
and
Victoria Radin

Series Editor: Mark Forstater

CORONET BOOKS
Hodder & Stoughton

A CIP catalogue record for this title is available
from the British Library

ISBN 0 340 73321 7 (hardback)
ISBN 0 340 73322 5 (paperback)

Printed and bound in Great Britain by Clays Ltd, St Ives plc

Hodder and Stoughton
A division of Hodder Headline
338 Euston Road
London NW1 3BH

DEDICATION

MF:

*To my parents
Max and Dorothy,
with gratitude for the precious gift.*

VR:

To Edward and Beatrice

Contents

Acknowledgements

MARK FORSTATER

I would like to thank the following for helping in the creation of this book and audiotape:

Rowena Webb, my editor at Hodder & Stoughton, who had the courage to commission this series.

Rupert Lancaster, Editor of Hodder Audio, for his support and help on the audio version.

David Roper of Heavy Entertainment for recording and editing the audio book.

David Troughton and Luisa Milwood-Haigh for an inspired reading of the audio book.

Maya, Pete, Suko and Jamie who read early drafts and gave valuable suggestions.

My agent Liv Blumer for all her help and support.

Victoria Radin for her fresh and original translations which have added immensely to the quality of the book.

Chris Norton for his mind map suggestion.

Faber and Faber Ltd for permission to quote from the play *Art* by Yasmina Reza.

And, as always, my wife Jo who continues to put up with all my nonsense.

Acknowledgements

Victoria Radin

I'd like to thank Seneca, an unlikely guide on the face of it, whose unrelenting reality principle and wild black humour helped me to reconcile myself to things I could not. I hope this little book will have a similar effect on others; and that Seneca's shade will not begrudge me my presumption in cutting up and reconfiguring his prose for the purpose of introducing him to new readers.

I also wish to acknowledge the translations of J. W. Basore and C. D. N. Costa, as well as Robin Campbell's abridged modern rendering of the Letters and E. Phillips Barkers' Herculean and marvellously rhetorical translation of the entire epistolary corpus, published in 1932, for enabling me to gain a multiple view of the work; though the liberties taken are my own.

Finally, I must thank Helen Campbell, who was kind enough to give up her Easter to copy-edit this manuscript.

It is to philosophy that we must look for the origins of civilisation.

CICERO

The gift of life comes from the heavens; the gift of living well from philosophy.

SENECA

PART ONE

The Rich Philosopher

Mark Forstater

Preface

The Death of Seneca

The writer, statesman and philosopher Lucius Annaeus Seneca was condemned to death on slender pretexts by three of the five Roman Emperors who ruled during his lifetime. Like a cat, he had several lives and managed to evade the first two sentences. The third, pronounced by the wild young Emperor Nero, who had once been Seneca's student, had to be undergone in the Roman manner of assassination by forced suicide.

The historian Tacitus described Seneca's last, ultimately botched moments in heroic if grisly detail.

PLACE: ROME
YEAR: 65

Nero asked if Seneca was prepared for death. An aide replied that the philosopher was calm and showed no signs of fear. This so enraged the Emperor that he made the death sentence immediate.

With complete calm, Seneca then asked for his will. This was refused. So Seneca turned to the friends gathered around him and said:

'Since I'm forbidden to show my gratitude to you for all your help, I shall leave you my sole remaining possession, and

13

my best. It's the pattern of my life. If you remember it, your friendship will be rewarded by your ability to do good.'

As he spoke he insisted they stop weeping and remain strong. He reminded them of their philosophy: where had it gone, with its resolutions to hold firm in adversity?

'Surely you weren't blind to the fact that Nero is cruel?' he demanded. 'After murdering his own mother and brother, it was inevitable that he would kill his moral teacher.'

These words were obviously intended for a wider audience.

Then Seneca embraced his young wife and, with a tenderness very different from his former demeanour, entreated her to curb her grief and find consolation in his well-spent life. But she insisted on dying with him. 'I advised you to find solace in life,' he said. 'If you prefer death and glory, we shall die together. But yours will be the nobler one, because it is by choice.'

Then, with a single incision, Seneca and Paulina cut their arms. But Seneca's aged body, thin from plain living, bled too feebly. So he also severed the veins in his legs.

The philosopher's death was slow. His doctor supplied poison; when it had no effect he was placed in a bath of warm water. Even now his presence of mind and humour had not deserted him, and he sprinkled a little of the bath water on the slaves around him, remarking that this was his offering to the gods. Finally he was carried into a steam bath. Here, at last, he died by suffocation.

His cremation took place without ceremony. Its simplicity was in accordance with his own instructions – which he had written when he was at the height of his power and wealth.

1

Fate and Fortune

It is one of those quirks of history that at the same time that Seneca was born in the far western end of the vast and sprawling Roman Empire, in the province of Spain, a Jewish boy named Yehoshua (better known to us as Jesus) was born in the far east, in the province of Judaea.

While Seneca was to rise to eminence and wealth as one of the three men ruling history's most powerful empire, Jesus was to live in obscurity and poverty and be killed like a slave.

Apart from their deaths at the hands of a barbaric and brutal Roman authority, what links these two contemporary figures is that both, in vastly different ways, were concerned with the state of our souls. Jesus was a Jewish prophet and Seneca a Stoic philosopher, but they both preached an ethical approach to life based on justice and the sanctity of life. Their teachings, Jewish and Stoic, two separate streams of thought, came together to form the ethical doctrine of Christianity, traditionally the main influence on our attitudes to conduct and behaviour.

Both men spent time in the wilderness. Jesus went into solitude to confront his demons and receive his calling. Seneca was sent into exile for eight years, and his writings show he had ample time to reflect on life. The

cause of Jesus' death was his attempt to overthrow
Roman power and reinstate a Jewish theocracy. He
became a revolutionary, and revolutionaries, if unsuccessful, often face a violent end. But Seneca was a writer
and orator without strong political leanings. He accepted
the powerful Empire that he was born into and which,
for five years, he co-ruled. Why was he forced to commit
suicide?

Seneca lived during a time of grotesque danger, insta-
bility, luxury and extravagance. It was an age of uncertainty, lacking common spiritual values. Confused,
people searched for both diverting entertainment and
emotional salvation. Immense riches and desperate
poverty jostled together in the same city of Rome. There
was a strong sense of cultural breakdown.

The parallels between his time and ours are many and
striking. We too live in an uncertain world, where natural disasters like floods, earthquakes, hurricanes and
fires, or terrifying new diseases like Aids, CJD or Ebola
can attack us unawares and destroy our lives. We are
frightened of the food we eat, the water we drink and the
air we breathe.

Uncontrolled savage wars erupt, creating enemies of
neighbours and bringing ethnic cleansing and genocide
close to home. Boy soldiers in Africa and Asia carry AK-
47s while other boys in America massacre their fellow
students with hand guns. Drive-by shootings, the hole in
the ozone layer, terrorism, mass migrations, serial killers,
the buying and selling of body organs, babies and sex
slaves give us a feeling of apocalypse now, a sense that
we are coming to the end of something, not the apoca-

lyptical end of time that the Jews and Christians expected 2,000 years ago, but the end of an era of relative stability.

Although Seneca lived 2,000 years ago, the story of his life appears remarkably modern. Like many of us, he was torn between conflicting ambitions, and the compromises he made in attempting to integrate them failed. He was split between two desires, badly wanting to be a player on the world's most powerful stage while hoping to live a philosophical life of tranquillity and contentment. This combination of the worldly and the sublime is a difficult balance for anyone to achieve.

Remarkably, Seneca managed to fulfil all his worldly desires: power, acclaim as a writer, and huge wealth. He was a man of great accomplishments and achievements. But the other side of his desire, the philosophical life, taught him that these achievements were ultimately empty, and that true virtue was to be found elsewhere. He saw too late that the karmic effects of his compromises destroyed the very tranquillity he wanted so badly.

What makes Seneca an interesting writer is his awareness of his own condition, his perception of his own flaws, his knowledge of the gulf between the often sordid, even despicable political acts he had to carry out, and the contemplative life that was his ideal. He could see clearly philosophy's blessed land, but his journey there was long, slow and painful, and finally he managed only a short stay. But his writings survived and have been read for 2,000 years, and they are as applicable today as they were two millennia ago.

In Yasmina Reza's play *Art* there is the following

dialogue:

SERGE: *By the way, have you read this?*

(He picks up De Vita Beata (The Happy Life) *by Seneca and throws it on to the low table just in front of Marc.)*

Read it, it's a masterpiece.

(Marc picks up the book, opens it and leafs through it.)

SERGE: *Incredibly modern. Read that, you don't need to read anything else.*

It is extraordinary that Seneca's writings are being rediscovered in our post-modern world. They comprise a number of moral essays, a set of philosophical letters, a book of natural science and eight tragedies, all of which were appreciated in Seneca's own time and rediscovered by the Italian Renaissance. His accessible and lively journalistic prose style was imitated by the essayists Montaigne and Bacon, and the stark violence, horror, bloodthirsty revenge and rhetorical dialogue of his tragedies had a great influence on Elizabethan dramatists, including Shakespeare and Marlowe.

Seneca believed that life was a constant struggle against the unpredictability of fate and Fortune. He lived with the constant expectation that existence was changeable and fickle, and that however rewarding and satisfying life might be at times, things could change drastically at any moment.

Seneca thought the only way to challenge these changes of Fortune was to become immune to their effects and not respond to them as people normally do. He tried to achieve this by following a philosophy, Stoicism, that altered his attitude to life and enabled him to react to loss in a different way from other people. Stoicism helped him acquire an inner state of freedom and peace that was intended to leave him untroubled and detached from pain, disappointment or failure.

Seneca observed that most people are seduced by the glittering appeal of life's material rewards – houses, possessions, money – into holding an irrational attitude to the world. When we are elated by gain and depressed by loss, our values become distorted and we begin to live a life of illusion, losing sight of the distinction between the true and the false.

In alienating ourselves from inner truth, our identities become tentative and uncertain, and we are easily swayed by the examples of others. We follow majority opinions and tastes rather than our deepest convictions. Many of us waste much of our time scrabbling to make money and achieve high status, failing to fulfil our potential for happiness. As we mistake the false for the true, attaching ourselves slavishly to material objects, our judgements about the world become suspect and we stray further and further from the truth. Increasingly confused and perplexed about what life means and how to get the best out of it, we often feel lost.

Seneca's mission was to create a practical, down-to-earth recipe for living that could alleviate these symptoms of spiritual illness and be applied in all circumstances. In doing this, he became the first self-help writer: his collection of *Philosophical Letters* is a manual covering subjects as diverse as enduring adversity, anger and noise pollution, living with anxiety and fear, finding happiness and tranquillity, friendship and coping with ageing, illness and death.

If Seneca's thoughts appear to us now as just 'common sense', it's because he was the prime source in our civilisation for many of these ideas. His thinking will not appear original and striking unless we make an historic leap and understand that in many cases it was his expression of these ideas that brought them into European consciousness.

If his writings are now undergoing a renaissance, it's because Seneca has something to tell us about our journey in the great global economy of the twenty-first century. As a Roman he was part of the first major wave of this international and cosmopolitan movement. Where Seneca went before, many of us will follow.

Early Days

Like many famous Romans, Seneca was not born in Rome. He was a native of Cordoba, the leading town in the Roman province of Spain where he was born around the year 4 BC.

Seneca's father, Marcus Annaeus Seneca, belonged to the knightly class and was a Roman procurator, or revenue collector. The elder Seneca was a well-known scholar of rhetoric, the art of public speaking and debate, a skill he passed on to his middle son.

The high social standing of the Seneca family was based on their ownership of extensive olive groves and vineyards, probably managed by Helvia, Seneca's mother. Seneca the elder had had ambitions to be a Roman Senator, but he never achieved that honour.

The Roman historian Sallust, in his preface to *The Catiline Conspiracy* shows the prevailing attitude of educated Romans to ambition.

Every man who wishes to rise superior to the lower animals should strive his hardest to avoid living all his days in silent obscurity, like the beasts of the field, creatures which go with their faces to the ground and are the slaves of their bellies.

We human beings have mental as well as physical powers; the mind, which we share with gods, is the ruling element in us, while the chief function of the body, which we have in common with the beasts, is to obey.

Surely, therefore, it is our intellectual rather than our physical powers that we should use in the pursuit of fame.

This was the route of Cicero, the great orator and lawyer, and it was the model for talented men like Seneca. These men were planning on becoming not famous warriors but celebrated speakers, thinkers and writers. This kind of celebrity often brought with it wealth, prestige, power and status.

The elder Seneca brought his son to Rome as a boy to groom him for a political life by studying rhetoric and philosophy, two Greek subjects that had become essential for all educated Romans. This gave Seneca an early interest in philosophy, and he was drawn initially to Pythagorean mysticism.

The Pythagoreans believed that the soul was immortal and that on death it could re-incarnate into another newly born creature. Since humans and animals had souls, both eating meat and performing animal sacrifices were anathema to the Pythagoreans. The teenage Seneca was captivated by this teaching and soon became a vegetarian.

The Emperor Tiberius had recently banned the Jews and other eastern sects from Rome, and Seneca the elder was concerned that people might assume his son's new diet was part of a religious conversion. He dissuaded Seneca from following the practice of vegetarianism, arguing that it would be bad for his political career. Seneca later toyed with Epicureanism before arriving at the Stoic philosophy that was so influential among Rome's educated classes.

Stoicism was a Greek philosophy that in Seneca's time was already 350 years old. It got its name from the *stoa*, or porch, at the market-place in Athens where Zeno of Citium taught. Zeno couldn't afford his own school, so he taught in the open air, and the porch provided shelter from the sun and rain.

Zeno's Stoicism was also a kind of spiritual shelter in that it aimed to help people adapt to life in society while still retaining the most important part of being human – the freedom of the mind. Chapter Two goes into more detail on Stoicism, but let me summarise it here by saying that it was a philosophy that gave the highest value to the individual, and asserted each person's right to control his or her own destiny. It was a philosophy that formed character and transformed souls.

Seneca started his career by filling some minor public offices, but then contracted tuberculosis and had to travel to Egypt for some years to recuperate. This serious illness afflicted him for his entire life.

My illness started when I was quite young. Later I declined so badly that I was nothing but catarrh, wasted to skin and bone. Many times I had the impulse to cut life short. Only the thought of my kind old father held me back. I didn't see my own courage in dying, but his courage broken by his loss of me, so I said to myself, 'You must live.' Sometimes even to live is an act of courage.

I'll tell you what comforted me in those days, stating first that the very thoughts in which I found rest proved as good as a cure. Pure consolations turn to healing medicine, and anything that supports the spirit does the body good too. The pursuit of Stoic wisdom was my salvation. That I left my sickbed and regained my strength I credit to philosophy. I owe her my life, and that's my smallest debt to her.

In Egypt Seneca used the facilities of the famous library at Alexandria to research the geography, geology, ethnology and marine life of Egypt and India. Taking advantage of the fact that his uncle was Prefect in Egypt, he gained valuable experience in Imperial administration and finance.

The Young Lawyer

Seneca returned from Egypt to Rome when he was thirty. After qualifying as a lawyer, he became a quaestor, a magistrate responsible for public finances. A year later he entered the Senate, rapidly became the leading speaker there, and started to make money and a reputation. Then, in AD 37, the mad and twisted twenty-five-year-old Caligula ascended the throne, and it became a dangerous time to be ambitious.

The Roman Empire of Seneca's time was a dictatorship, with power concentrated in the hands of one man. This system was put into place by the first emperor, Augustus Caesar, the heir and nephew of Julius Caesar. Augustus had set up a regime that looked on the surface like a constitutional government, with the Senate and the people playing their traditional roles and making important decisions of state. But this was only an illusion, since the real power always resided with Augustus and his few advisers and cronies. He had the power of the army behind him, and this, as always, was the key to Imperial rule.

With Augustus all political debate in Rome came to an end, and people settled into the long and prosperous Pax Romana, when Roman power cleansed the roads and seas of bandits and pirates, leaving land owners, traders and tax collectors free to get on with the real business of making money. Their economic system was underpinned by having huge numbers of slaves available to do all the difficult work on farms and in workshops, mines and domestic houses.

This political system worked well enough as long as the emperor was a sensible ruler, but Augustus' (family) successors had characters that were often bizarre, low or corrupt. Roman history shows that power concentrated in the hands of a few generally corrupts those few, and the absolute power of emperors can corrupt them absolutely. The greater the power of Caesar, the greater the fear he could provoke. Fear and unexpressed hatred became the dominant atmosphere in Rome when a perverse and omnipotent ruler like Caligula was on the throne.

Caligula's regime started well, but after seven months he came down with a mysterious illness. When he recovered, his personality had changed drastically. His behaviour was now peculiar and unpredictable, and he seemed to have no control over his impulses and desires. He began to order Senators to be whipped, and instigated a regime of torture using wooden and metal implements. He became wildly extravagant and once spent the entire tax revenue of three provinces on a single meal.

Caligula shocked the Romans by marrying one of his sisters, Drusilla, even though she was already married. He declared that he and Drusilla were gods and, since gods were superior to ordinary humans, they had the right to kill and torture anyone who offended them. Caligula became a charming murderer. He invited the relatives of those he killed to join him for supper that same day to make certain they enjoyed themselves. If he saw that they were unhappy, they too could be despatched. He became a hated and despised figure but declared, 'Let them hate me, as long as they fear me!'

It is said that Caligula, insecure and obsessively jealous of anyone with talent, ordered Seneca's death after the lawyer had made a brilliant prosecution speech. Seneca's life was saved by one of Caligula's mistresses, who argued that he was not worth killing since he was nearly dead of tuberculosis anyway. Although the records are not clear, Seneca must have decided that politics under Caligula was unhealthy, and he seems to have taken leave of public life to spend some time writing.

Now began the see-saw effects of Fortune, those extreme leaps and falls that contributed so strongly to the arc of Seneca's life.

You take life on the same terms as the public bath, the crowd or the journey. Sometimes things will be thrown at you, and sometimes they'll hit you. To live is not a dainty business. You've started on a long road: you must have slides and bumps and falls, and get tired and sigh for death (what a pose!), and leave a companion behind at one place, bury a friend elsewhere, and be afraid of someone somewhere else: you've a rough road to travel and it's full of bumps like these.

Caligula had been in power for only four years when his excesses goaded his enemies into assassinating him. His successor, Claudius, managed virtually to buy the throne by bribing the Praetorian Guards, the troop of 10,000 soldiers based near Rome whose job was to guard the emperor and the city.

The middle-aged Claudius, one of whose pastimes was watching scenes of torture and death, soon accused Seneca of adultery with another of Caligula's sisters, condemned him without a trial, and exiled him to the bleak island of Corsica.

Fall and Rise

Given the state of Seneca's health, exile to Corsica was a dreadful punishment. The barren island was scorching in summer, bitterly cold in winter, rugged and infertile. Seneca was overwhelmed by his misfortunes, which no amount of Stoic philosophy could repair. He had only recently buried his young son, and while he was in exile his first wife also died. But these terrible years gave him time to think and write, and it was during his stay in Corsica that the philosophical Seneca began to emerge. Exile made him into a philosopher.

Alone, he attempted (Stoically) to convince himself that exile was not an evil but an opportunity. He wrote a moving Consolation to his mother.

Within twenty days of burying my son, who died as you held and kissed him, you heard that I had been taken away. Now you say, 'I am deprived of my dearest son's embrace. I can no longer enjoy seeing him or talking to him. Where is the one whose appearance calmed my troubled brow, to whom I confided all my troubles? Where are the conversations of which I never tired?'

Seneca explained, not altogether convincingly, that to a Stoic exile is just a change of residence, and that living in isolation, poverty and disgrace is no hardship as long as freedom of mind is retained.

An exile's poverty brings no hardship. For no place of exile is so barren that it can't abundantly support a man. It's the mind that creates our wealth, and this goes with us into exile, and in the harshest desert places it finds enough to nourish the body and revels in the enjoyment of its own goods.

He used his freedom to write tragedies, poems and essays, including a grovelling Consolation to Polybius, one of Claudius' powerful freed slaves, on the death of the freedman's son, which included an embarrassing and unsuccessful plea to the Emperor to pardon him.

Seneca's luck turned in AD 49 after Claudius executed his wife Messalina and took a new wife, Caligula's third sister Agrippina. She persuaded Claudius to bring Seneca back to Rome after eight painful years, made him Praetor (a high magistrate just below Consul), and employed him as chief tutor to her twelve-year-old son, Nero. Following banishment and disgrace, Seneca now found himself a trusted mentor in the world's most powerful family.

Agrippina was a ruthless and ambitious woman obsessed with power and money. Intelligent and attractive, she was willing to do anything to obtain ultimate power in Rome. The daughter of a war hero and the granddaughter of Augustus Caesar, she had been raised surrounded by power and adulation. She had been the sister of an emperor and was now the wife of another. But as a woman in a male-dominated society, the only role available to her was that of wife or mother. Roman society would never allow her to hold ultimate power on her own. The only way open to her was to manipulate people and events so that her young son could be adopted as Claudius' successor – as the Emperor's mother she would be able to wield power in his place. She completely dominated and manipulated Nero and used him ruthlessly.

Agrippina was no fan of philosophy but she had a number of considered reasons for employing Seneca. First, because of his literary fame, she hoped to gain popularity from bringing him home. Second, she believed that he would become a reliable adviser and ally in her plans for future power. Third, his name and reputation would lend prestige to Nero. Finally, she knew she could count on his loyalty because he owed her his freedom and his life.

Agrippina had made Seneca an offer he could not refuse. There was no real choice between death in exile or life – however strange and dangerous – at the royal court. Seneca must have convinced himself that the chance to teach this cowed and perverse young man to develop leadership qualities, though a difficult challenge, was not impossible. His job was to transform Nero from the impulsive, insecure, fearful and dependent boy that his mother had made him, into a more stable and sensible adult.

Nero had no interest in politics and empire but loved art and horses. He learned to play the cithara, a kind of lyre, to write and sing songs, declaim poetry, paint and sculpt, and ride four horse-chariots. Running an empire was the last thing on his mind; being an artist, an actor and singer was his primary interest.

The Power Broker

When Claudius was sixty-four and Nero seventeen, Agrippina made her calculated move. One night at dinner Claudius suddenly became ill after eating his favourite dish of cooked mushrooms. The ancient historians agree that Agrippina must have plotted his death; they even mention the name of Locasta, the woman who supplied the poison. With Claudius dead Agrippina managed the difficult and unpredictable transfer of power when she called on Afranius Burrus, the Commander of the Praetorian Guard, to declare her seventeen-year-old son emperor. Agrippina knew she could count on this ex-soldier to support Nero because she had given him his job. Not only that, she had appointed many of the officers serving under him. And to keep the troops happy she had Nero offer them a healthy bribe, just as his uncle Claudius had done.

Now the most powerful empire of the ancient world found itself ruled by a seventeen-year-old boy. Agrippina, having achieved her lifelong aim, installed herself next to him, ready to rule.

Seneca and Burrus, who had worked together as part of Agrippina's team, now found themselves, as 'friends' of Nero, in powerful positions. But they faced a dilemma. Should they support Agrippina, to whom they owed personal loyalty, or should they try to aid Nero to take on responsibility and power as rightful emperor? They knew that Nero was so completely dominated by his mother as to have no initiative of his own, and was used to being led by her. But there would come a time when the boy would grow into a man and attempt to assert himself. Did they want to be on his side or his mother's when that day came?

They distrusted Agrippina and knew that her rule would be worse than her son's, provided that Nero allowed his two 'friends' to advise him. Seneca and Burrus needed to devise a system whereby Nero was in nominal power but all the key decisions were made by a council of advisers. Since Agrippina was a member of this council, Seneca suggested to Nero that all the members offer their advice in written form, so that the Emperor could privately choose which to follow. In this way Seneca managed to keep the meddlesome Agrippina from dominating Nero and from discovering the policies of the other advisers. Agrippina must have been furious that this ex-tutor, with no constitutional position, was so influential at court.

Keeping her away from public affairs was no easy task. She travelled around Rome in a litter surrounded by her own military guard and had asked the Senate to meet in the Imperial palace so that she could listen to the debates from behind a curtain. The key moment in this power-play came when an Armenian delegation arrived in Rome to meet the Emperor. Nero was seated on his throne when Agrippina entered the room to take her place next to him. Seneca whispered something to the young Emperor, who got up to greet his mother and led her away.

Agrippina was enraged. She had spent most of her life plotting to gain the Empire, and now that she had finally succeeded she was being sidelined by the two men she had installed as her aides. 'I made you Emperor' she is reported to have shouted at her son, and she used every means to win him over and keep him within her control. All the ancient historians claim that her control over Nero arose from an incestuous relationship and it was by sexual means that she managed to keep him dependent on her.

Although Seneca had not been engaged to teach Nero philosophy, the first few years of his reign show Stoic influences. Seneca wrote all Nero's speeches, and the first one that he delivered to the Senate was full of conciliatory ideas and respect for the Senate's prestige. Seneca wrote these words, 'I do not carry with me any hatreds, any resentments, any thirst for vengeance.' If Seneca had anything to do with it, Nero's regime was not going to be a repeat of treasonous murder trials, torture and military adventures, but one of reconciliation.

Seneca also wrote an essay addressed to Nero, 'On Mercy', in which he uses flattery in an attempt to woo the young ruler to fairness and justice. He was trying to teach Nero that the Stoic way, the way of the wise man, can lead to a better society, one ruled with love and affection rather than by fear. In the essay he made Nero aware of the power that the emperor wields.

I am the judge of life and death for all nations. In my power is the destiny and status of every man. By my lips fortune proclaims what gifts she means each one to have... At my nod, those many thousands of swords restrained by my peace shall be drawn. Mine is the right to decree which nations shall be utterly destroyed, which dispersed, which given freedom or deprived of it, which kings shall become slaves, whose heads shall be crowned with honour, which cities razed to the ground, and which shall rise again.

Seneca explained to Nero the attitude that the Stoic wise man, their ideal person, would adopt towards his fellow citizens, if he wielded this absolute personal power.

The wise man will aid, will benefit, and since he is born to be of help to everyone and to serve the common good, he will give to each an equal share. He will extend a due measure of his goodness even to those unfortunates who deserve to be rebuked and disciplined; but much more gladly will he come to the rescue of the distressed and those struggling with adversity.

Whenever he can, he will fight off the battering of Fortune; for in what way can he make better use of his resources or his strength than in restoring what chance has overthrown? And, too, he will not avert his gaze or his sympathy from anyone because he has a withered leg, or is emaciated and in rags, or is old and leans on a stick. But everyone who is worthy he will aid, and will, like a god, look graciously on the unfortunate.

A prince should be to his subjects as he wishes the gods to be to himself.

This fine advice to a sovereign remained influential for many hundreds of years, and it was eventually studied by Queen Elizabeth I, who read Seneca as part of her education.

That Nero initially followed these ideas is shown in his attitude to the gladiatorial contests, where he insisted, against the audience's wishes, on eliminating the wholesale slaughter of criminals and slaves.

Agrippina's Slide

Having made successful speeches (written by Seneca) in the Senate, and publicly demonstrated that he could stand up to his mother, Nero grew bolder and more independent. In what may have been the first important act he ever accomplished by himself and on his own behalf, he fell totally in love with an older woman, Claudia Acté. But this beautiful twenty-five-year-old was not an obvious Imperial consort – Nero's first choice as a lover was a freed slave girl who worked in the palace as a servant.

Knowing Seneca's attitude to slavery makes this choice less surprising.

The man you call your slave was born of the same seed, has the same good sky above him, breathes as you do, lives as you do, dies as you do! Treat your slave with kindness, with courtesy, too. Let him share your conversation, your deliberation and your company. A man gives himself his character; his employment chance bestows.

The philosopher was the first ancient writer to attack slavery. Like all Stoics, he believed in the equality of all peoples and our common brotherhood. We take these ideas for granted because they are embedded in our contemporary ideology and way of life, but in the ancient world few shared them. Even a great thinker like Aristotle believed in a basic inequality: some were naturally born to rule and others were by nature born to be slaves.

Seneca and Burrus must have been pleased that the Emperor had found further distraction from the cares of office, and they set Acté up in an apartment where the lovers could meet. To prevent Agrippina from knowing, Seneca's relative Annaeus Serenus pretended to be her lover, bringing expensive gifts and paying the rent.

Once Agrippina found out about this liaison she raged with jealousy. A few years before, when she was married to Claudius, she had arranged a dynastic marriage for Nero, then aged fifteen, with Octavia, Claudius' thirteen-year-old-daughter. Octavia was now Nero's Empress, but he wanted to replace her with Acté.

Agrippina bitterly opposed the affair and told Nero that she would never accept it. But she underestimated the seriousness of his feelings for the girl, and when he threatened to abdicate and take Acté into exile with him, Agrippina realised her opposition was alienating her son. Now she backtracked and offered the lovers the use of her bedroom.

Nero knew his mother had no real love for him, but cared only for her own standing. Wanting to be free of her control, he used the excuse of her having so many visitors to suggest that she would have more room if she left the palace. When she moved out, he redeployed his troops and took away her contingent of guards. It was clear to everyone that Agrippina had lost influence, and that Seneca and Burrus were now the powers behind the throne.

Nero had had a taste of his own might, however, and as he matured he began to exhibit the perverse and impulsive behaviour that would win him his reputation as a corrupt and criminal tyrant.

High Life, Low Lives

Nero was only eighteen and had led a strangely sheltered existence. From being an overprotected, overindulged child he was thrust into the position of a virtual god to his 100 million subjects. He had never had a chance to live a normal life, and now he wanted to get together with his young friends and do what most adolescents enjoy: go out on the town.

But when you're the Emperor, with your face on every coin, it's not so simple. Nero took to slipping out of the palace disguised as a slave, in company with four or five friends.

What they got up to on these nocturnal ramblings is described very well by Tacitus:

Disguised as a slave, Nero ranged the streets, brothels and bars with his friends, who stole goods from shops and attacked passers by. Their identity was unsuspected: indeed, as marks on his face testified, Nero himself had been hit. When it became known that the leader of these hooligans was the Emperor, street attacks on people multiplied. Since this violent behaviour was tolerated, other young 'Neros' soon mobilised gangs and behaved in the same way, with complete impunity. Rome at night came to resemble a defeated city.

One night Nero and his band attacked a Senator, Julius Montanus, who hit back at them and injured the Emperor. Discovering the next day who he had beaten, Montanus sent an apology, but his apology was interpreted as a slur, and he was forced to commit suicide.

This didn't stop Nero from carousing, but now he and his low life friends went out shadowed by soldiers and gladiators, who intervened whenever the gang's victims looked like putting up a fight. The old Roman atmosphere of cruelty, fear and terror was returning.

Seneca on Trial

While Nero enjoyed himself with art, Acté and bar crawls, Seneca and Burrus between them managed to produce a number of years of unequalled good government. Their authority did not derive from any legal or constitutional role but was solely based on Nero's willingness to let his old tutor deal with matters which he considered too boring. This enabled the two counsellors to introduce substantial legal and financial reforms, including a reduction of indirect taxation and steps to prevent extortion and fraud by provincial governors. They fought a successful war in Armenia to secure the eastern frontier, and Seneca indulged his geographical interests by sending an expedition to search for the source of the Nile. He also revised the Roman system of shorthand.

In AD 56, Seneca was made Consul, and reached the height of his ambition. He was virtually co-ruler of the Empire, and this position enabled him to amass enormous wealth, through inheritances, gifts from Nero, and by lending money, since Seneca could invest securely through inside knowledge of state policy. Inevitably a number of accusations and slanders came flying his way:

he was accused of having slept with Agrippina; claims were made that he introduced Nero to pederasty; complaints were made about the uselessness of his studies and the artificiality of his oratorical style.

But the main attack on him was for having acquired one of the largest fortunes (300 million sesterces) of his time. Seneca owned some of the best vineyards in Italy, beautiful estates and gardens, and reputedly hosted banquets of prodigious extravagance. At the same time, he claimed that his own personal life-style was one of hard beds, cold baths, daily runs, simple food and no alcohol.

Nero made a habit of giving villas and land holdings that he had inherited to his friends and associates. Seneca was one of the favoured few who received an estate or gardens as a token of the Emperor's friendship. Sometimes these had belonged to people Nero was thought to have killed, like his stepbrother Britannicus and his aunt Domitia Lepida.

It could be argued that Seneca should have turned such gifts down. But could he have rejected them, coming as they did from so powerful and unstable an employer? To refuse such gifts would have been tantamount to saying to Nero, 'I don't approve of how you acquired this estate or had it given to you. It would be wrong for me to accept any gifts that come from your hands.'

Seneca had this to say on the subject:

To refuse a gift is to make an enemy of an insolent monarch, who would have everything that he gives valued at a high rate. It doesn't matter whether you're unwilling to give to a king or to receive from him, the offence is equal in either case, or rather even worse in the latter, since to the proud it's more bitter to be disdained than not to be feared.

It is also not surprising that Seneca was so good at making money. He was groomed to know how to handle it and learned from an early age how it was made. He was also in the right position to do so easily, and as a result it flowed like an undammed river.

In just a few years Seneca had exchanged penniless exile for the life of a rich and powerful Senator, money-lender and landowner, yet his view of himself was as an ascetic and scholarly Stoic philosopher. His accusers said he was a hypocrite who, like most philosophers, did not practise what he preached.

Stoicism regarded money and possessions as 'indifferent' or neutral things, not worthy of being desired or pursued. How could a Stoic become one of the richest men in the Empire?

Stoicism also had a long tradition of speaking out strongly against political tyranny, yet here was Seneca acting as chief political adviser to the violent Emperor Nero. Surely, his enemies said, this was too great a contradiction. Seneca wanted the reputation of a man of wisdom and spirit while enjoying a corrupt worldly success.

Seneca reacted by writing an essay called 'The Happy Life', which starts as a treatise about happiness and ends as an apologia for his own wealth. He defends himself by saying that he harmed no one in becoming rich, and that money is not the basis of his personal happiness. If he lost all his money he would still be capable of leading a happy life. He agrees that no one fully practises what they preach but that philosophy is an ideal to which one must aspire.

Seneca believed, in accordance with Stoic thinking, that true happiness is founded only on virtue. Although few of us think in these terms any more, most people agree that it is better to pursue good than evil. We can probably identify with a number of Seneca's views on happiness, such as the following.

True happiness is founded on virtue. And what advice does virtue gives you? That you should not consider anything either a good or an evil that is not the result of either virtue or vice. Then, that you should be unconcerned both in the face of evil and by the enjoyment of good, to the end that – as far as it's possible – you may embody God.

And what does virtue promise you for this undertaking? Mighty privileges and equality to the divine. You will not be held back by constraint, you will lack nothing, you will be free, safe, unhurt. There is nothing that you can try in vain, and nothing will be refused you. Everything will happen according to your desire, nothing adverse will occur, and nothing contrary to your expectations and wishes.

For if a person is placed beyond the reach of any desire, what can he possibly lack? If a person has gathered all that is his, what need does he have of any outside thing?

Seneca was able to defend himself because he felt that his role as Nero's adviser was a valuable one for the state, and that his own wealth and power were not obtained corruptly. He did not feel that his philosophy was compromised by his position or the actions he had taken. But this sort of innocence was soon to change, when Nero committed one of the most famous crimes in history, and Seneca was left to clean up after him and pay the spiritual and mortal consequences.

Agrippina's Cruise

In AD 58, when Nero was twenty, he fell in love for the second time. He was still in a loveless marriage to Octavia and had Acté as his loyal mistress, when he met the new wife of his nocturnal companion Marcus Salvius Otho. Her name was Poppaea Sabina, and she was a famous beauty.

Poppaea Sabina, who was in her mid-twenties, had luxurious auburn hair and delicate white skin which she kept in perfect condition by bathing in asses' milk. It is said that she kept a herd of 500 asses just for that purpose. She came from a rich and powerful family, and no doubt thought that being an empress would suit her extravagant tastes perfectly. Although she was newly married, she and Nero hit it off at once.

To clear the way for some serious adultery, Nero appointed his friend Otho as Governor of Lusitania (pres -ent day Portugal), which was then considered the far edge of the world. Now Nero had Poppaea all to himself, but she proved to be as difficult and haughty as she was glamorous. She thought Nero's association with Acté was degrading, and forced him to convert the ex-slave-girl from lover into friend. To his credit, Nero continued to support her financially.

But this was not enough for Poppaea. Her ambition was to become Empress of Rome, and Octavia was in the way, supported by Agrippina. Agrippina had not let her forced departure from the palace deter her from her aims. She would often turn up at the palace at noon to see Nero, to caress him, coddle him, smother him with affection, nag and wheedle from him whatever it was she wanted. And Nero was unable to turn her down. Her power over him was still great, and if she didn't get her way, she could call in enough favours and pay enough bribes to ensure that others would pester him on her behalf. With Agrippina still influencing Nero, there was no way Poppaea would replace Octavia. She mocked Nero and called him a mother's boy for still being under her power. How could he be the ruler of Rome when he couldn't even rule his own mother?

We can never know what finally makes someone decide to kill his own mother, but at some time during that year, the frustrated Nero took that incredible decision. As he grew older he grew more and more intolerant of restraint. He wanted to be free to do as he pleased, and with Agrippina alive he believed that would never happen. But how to kill her? He couldn't involve either Seneca or Burrus, because both of them would have advised against the idea. Instead Nero gathered a small band of trusted conspirators to work out the best plan.

There were few options. The Praetorian Guard loved Agrippina because of her heroic ancestry and would never take part. She could not be poisoned because she was paranoid about assassination and took antidotes as a precaution. She also made certain she was never alone so no dagger-wielding killer could obtain access to her.

Late that year or early the next, however, Nero attended a naval gladiatorial show which took place on a purpose-built artificial lake. The show included a unique ship that broke apart, dropping the animals on board into the water, and then closed up and sailed on. This technological marvel gave Nero the idea of how to construct the perfect murder weapon – a collapsing boat.

Nero approached the Commander of the Fleet, Anicetus, a freed Greek slave who had been one of his earliest tutors, and whom Nero had raised to prominence. He asked Anicetus to build a small boat that could collapse on top of his mother and kill her off. It would be the Emperor's job to arrange to get her on to the boat.

The plot was put in place during the holiday festival of Minerva. Nero was in the habit of leaving Rome to stay at his seaside villa at the Bay of Baiae, part of the Bay of Naples. He knew Agrippina would be holidaying at her villa nearby, and one dark and moonless night he arranged for her to come over for dinner. Tacitus says that she had heard rumours of a plot against her and was even more wary than usual.

Agrippina arrived with her lady-in-waiting, Acerronia Polla, and her bodyguard, Creperius Gallus, and Nero invited her in for a lavish dinner at which an abundance of wine was served. He was warm and affectionate to his mother and when she left at midnight he kissed her goodbye. Satisfied at being reconciled with Nero, she and her party boarded the boat and pushed off from the shore.

This was the start of a string of truly appalling events. The rest of the naval incident is told so well by Tacitus that I will quote his version.

Her bodyguard, Creperius Gallus, stood near the tiller. Her lady-in-waiting, Acerronia, leant over the feet of her resting mistress, happily talking about Nero's remorseful behaviour and his mother's re-established influence.

Then came the signal. Under the pressure of heavy lead weights, the roof caved in. Creperius was crushed and died instantly. Agrippina and Acerronia were saved by the raised sides of their couch, which was strong enough to hold the weight. The ship itself listed but didn't sink.

In the confusion, those in the conspiracy were hampered by the ones who were not. Some of the sailors had the idea of throwing their weight on one side to capsize the ship, but they took so long to improvise the plan that others had leant their weight on the other side.

Acerronia, whether on her own account or at Agrippina's suggestion, made the mistake of crying out 'I am Agrippina! Help, help the Emperor's mother!' She was immediately attacked and killed by blows from poles, oars and whatever ship's gear was handy.

In the confusion and turmoil, Agrippina kept quiet and tried to hide. Though she had an injury to her shoulder she slipped into the water and swam until she came to some fishing boats. They brought her to the Lucrine lake, from which she was taken home.

Agrippina knew that there had been a plot, not a shipwreck. She decided her only hope would be to profess ignorance, and she sent a messenger to Nero to inform him that she had survived a serious accident. The messenger was instructed to say to Nero that she needed rest and that no visit was necessary.

When Anicetus told Nero that Agrippina had escaped, the Emperor panicked. He imagined his mother arming her slaves to attack him, or rushing to the Senate to incriminate him. In the midst of his fear and confusion he didn't know what to do, so he woke Seneca and Burrus and told them what had happened. Tacitus relates:

For a long time neither spoke. They did not want to dissuade and be rejected. They may have felt that matters had gone so far that Nero had to strike before Agrippina, or die himself.

Seneca's ambition and the course of his life had now brought him to a moral turning point. It was not other people's morality that concerned him, but his own personal ethics, based on the Stoic ideas of good and evil. Pursuing the good led to moral excellence, whereas contamination by evil led to degradation and shame.

Now the years of compromise, the attempts to marry an ideal of philosophy with the realities of human power and weakness, the twists and turns of his own fate and Fortune, which had brought him from contempt and despair to riches and status, all came to a climax for Seneca. The diverse circumstances of his sixty-three years, the intertwining webs of his destiny, now all condensed down to this single moment in a seaside villa.

Two people had been killed, a terrible crime had been

committed, and the way of the world dictated that another would have to be undertaken, not by an impulsive and distorted young man, but by two mature and wise counsellors. Whatever history says about Seneca, it was in this defining moment that he came to realise for himself where his life of compromise had inevitably brought him. He had been willing to get his hands dirty; he did not expect to get them bloody as well. Tacitus continues:

Finally, Seneca turned to Burrus and asked if the troops should be ordered to kill her. Burrus replied that the Guard were devoted to the whole imperial house and would commit no violence against them. Anicetus must finish what he had begun. The Fleet Commander agreed, and Nero said, 'Go quickly! And take men who obey orders scrupulously!'

Now Nero let Agrippina's messenger in. While the ex-slave delivered the message, the Emperor dropped a short sword at his feet and, shouting that he was being attacked, had the man arrested. Now he could pretend that his mother had plotted against him, had been detected, and, in shame, had committed suicide.

Tacitus continues the sordid tale:

As soon as people had heard about Agrippina's terrible accident they ran to the beach, or climbed on to the embankment, or on to fishing boats nearby. Others waded out as far as they could, waving their arms. Huge crowds gathered with lights. The whole shore echoed with wails and prayers and the noise of all kinds of questions and ignorant answers. When she was known to be safe, they prepared to make a show of rejoicing.

But a menacing armed column arrived and dispersed them. Anicetus and his men surrounded the house and broke down the door. Arresting every slave in his path, he came to her bedroom door.

Here stood a few servants – the rest had been frightened away by the invasion. In her dimly lit room a single maid waited with Agrippina. Her alarm had increased as no one, not even her messenger, came from her son. If things had been well there wouldn't be this terribly ominous isolation, and then this sudden uproar.

Her maid vanished. 'Are you leaving me, too?' called Agrippina. Then she saw Anicetus, and behind him a naval captain and lieutenant. 'If you've come to visit, you can report that I'm better. But if you're assassins, I know my son is not responsible. He didn't order his mother's death.' The murderers slowly surrounded her bed and the captain swung a club and hit her on the head. Then as the lieutenant drew his sword to finish her off, she pointed to her womb and cried out: 'Strike here!' Blow after blow fell and she died.

The Aftermath

Nero sent a letter to the Senate explaining that Agrippina committed suicide as a result of her plot against the Emperor's life. Seneca, the eminent writer and philosopher, drafted the document. While it was being read out, one Senator, the Stoic Thrasea Paetus, stood up and walked out in silent protest.

Many years before, Seneca's father has written quite prophetically to his youngest son:

Your brothers are ambitious, and are preparing themselves for
a career in which even success has its dangers. Dangerous
though it is, I have urged your brothers to pursue it, so far at
least as they can do so within the strictest limits of honour.

For Seneca, honour was suddenly in short supply.

Three years later Burrus died and Seneca's position
weakened. By now Nero was listening to other advisers
and letting his violent and impulsive side have freer rein.
No doubt his new friends told him tales of Seneca's
wealth and growing popularity, and painted him as a
dangerous rival. Seneca, realising his position was
untenable, asked Nero to let him retire from public
affairs, and he tried to return all the wealth he had
acquired.

Nero eventually let him go, and Seneca was able to
withdraw from politics and for three years follow the
philosophical life he had so long desired. He and his second wife Paulina left Rome and travelled around Italy.
Seneca wrote daily, completing a number of essays and
the work he considered his philosophical and spiritual
legacy – the *Philosophical Letters*.

In AD 65 there was a conspiracy against Nero, and it
is certainly possible that Seneca had a hand in this plot.
He was considered by some of the conspirators as the
best possible replacement for the Emperor. After the plot
was discovered, many people lost their lives, including
Seneca, his brothers and his nephew Lucan, the celebrated poet. Virtually the entire male Seneca clan was
wiped out.

But the real reason Seneca was killed was because Nero was aware of how far he had drifted from his tutor's teachings, and he knew what Seneca thought of him. The Emperor had more than enough reasons to suffer a guilty conscience and had to kill Seneca to remove his silent criticism. Besides, Seneca knew too much about Nero's crimes, and like anyone who knows too much, had to die.

We see in Seneca a man much like our own contemporaries: educated and talented, he wanted to use his skills to make his way in the world, to become someone of note, and this ambition carried with it a desire for power and wealth. After all, for most of our recorded history it is this desire that has propelled men to achieve prominence in society.

To become famous and powerful, to have wealth and to acquire all the things that wealth promises – possessions, leisure, sexual opportunities and so on – are the motivational forces that drive many of us on. These are the desires that society approves of, and the media and our peers often expect of us. Many people dedicate themselves to a pursuit of material goals, to satisfy longings for self-aggrandisement, for the envy attached to name and possessions, and to achieve the immortality that fame promises.

In his *Letters* Seneca managed to transcend the painful acts he witnessed and helped to cover up. He acknowledges his faults and tells us how in daily practice he tries to live a life of harmony and health.

I feel that I'm being not only reformed, but transformed. But I still have many qualities which stand in need of concentration, elimination or development. And the very fact that my spirit can discern its own failings, of which it was ignorant before, is in itself evidence of its transformation for the better. Sometimes the sick must be congratulated because they themselves have recognized their illness.

I never spend an idle day. I even claim half the night for study. I've no time for sleep: I only succumb to it, my eyes, weary and blinking with tiredness, still riveted to my work. I've withdrawn not only from men, but from business, especially my own.

I'm working now for posterity, writing down some thoughts which may be of use to them. I'm committing to paper, like sovereign prescriptions, certain wholesome advice, effective, as I have found, in the case of my own sores, which, if they're not completely cured, have at least stopped spreading. I'm pointing out to others the right path which I've discovered late in life, when I'm already weary from wandering. I cry out to them, 'Avoid everything that pleases the crowd, avoid the gifts of chance. Stop dead at every accidental stroke of luck, in a spirit of doubt and alarm. It's hope of some kind that lures beast and bird to their death. Do you call these the 'gifts' of Fortune? They are snares!'

Cling to a sane and wholesome rule of life, indulging your body no more than good health demands. You must treat it rigorously in case it disobeys the spirit. Eat to satisfy your hunger, drink to quench your thirst, clothe yourself to keep out the cold, make your house a protection against personal harm. It doesn't matter if it's built of turf or of coloured marble. A straw roof, I assure you, shelters us no worse than a gold one.

Reflect that nothing deserves admiration but the spirit, which admits no greatness but its own.

He leaves us in the *Letters* a method and recipe for achieving mental health, and a way of looking at the world with reason and compassion. It is significant that many Roman emperors began their regimes well but soon degenerated into tyrants and despots. Seneca managed to change that pattern in his own life. After starting well, he too failed to live up to his ideals, but in the last three years of his life he managed to progress spiritually and to return to a new awareness. It was Seneca's Stoicism that enabled him to reclaim our admiration for him.

2

Philosophy as a Way of Life

The received idea about Stoicism is that it is a highly rational, repressive and emotionless response to life, a way of coping with experience by not expressing feelings, uncomplainingly enduring whatever happens to us. It appears as a philosophy that deals well with the harsher aspects of life, but not with the joyful parts.

This is not how the Roman Stoics saw their philosophy. They regarded life as a unique and unexpected gift of nature which made daily existence, if you knew how to let it, become a wonderful celebration, a festival of life. They believed that making the right judgements about life and following the moral good could provide a real joy and happiness.

This true moral good was found in following nature, and since nature has given us an intellectual facility, we have a need for contemplation and understanding as part of our way of life. It is true that Seneca, because his life was so influenced by the fickleness of Fortune, came to see existence as a fierce struggle against Fortune's whims. He believed that Stoicism gave its followers the ability to rise above Fortune, to avoid being harmed by it.

The Stoics believed in a rational god, a rational world and a rational mind. They followed good rather than evil because it was more reasonable to do so. But they under-stood that there are times when rationality becomes eclipsed by irrationality, and they called this irrationality the 'passions' that take hold of us and take us over.

These passions – strong, unlimited desires, emotions and irrational fears – are the cause of our disturbances and suffering. They bring on anxieties and worries that prevent us from living a free and happy life. Seneca sees philosophy as a therapy of the soul that enables its fol-lowers to deal with these passions and in the process to transform both their way of looking at the world and of acting in it.

Today we say that the passions and other irrational states are products of the unconscious mind, the hidden part of the brain that originates the many actions that we don't control. The Stoics believed that we have more rational control over our minds than we actually do. Because of the studies of Freud and Jung we believe that there is a greater limitation to reason and that the springs of our impulses lie deeply hidden.

We have a problem with the term 'reason', which implies a linear and abstract form of thinking that does not reflect the fullness and richness of imagination and feeling. But if we replace reason with the term 'con-sciousness', we are able to see that the Stoic mind is holistic and ecological, one that can be in tune with our contemporary modes of thought. Because Stoicism is pre-Christian, we can look at its ethical stance without the bias of a Christian viewpoint and judge it on the basis of its practicality for delivering a positive and beneficial attitude to life. If it is life enhancing and can lead to personal happiness, then it is a philosophy that can be effective in our new century.

To Seneca, reason was god: the *logos*, a fiery burning substance (almost like the burning bush but without the bush) that gave a rational and beneficial order to the world. The *logos* was also Nature and Fate, and through an endless chain of cause and effect its intelligence led to a predetermined and unalterable order of events in the world. Such a belief would normally lead to an extreme fatalism, where there would be no possibility of the individual altering his fate. Everything would be fixed and determined, and there would be no scope for individual freedom of will.

But, and here is one of the great paradoxes of Senecan and Stoic thought, and the reason why it has effective power, the Stoics also believed that each person who has reason and uses it is able through their individual will to make daily decisions about how best to live, to make choices about values, and to determine what they will seek and what they will avoid. In other words, Seneca's Stoic system believes in a form of free will as well as in a completely deterministic and fated universe.

If Seneca believed only in fate, individual will would count for nothing. If everything is predetermined, there would be no reason to make individual decisions or choices. Everything would happen as it was fated or planned to happen no matter what individual action you took.

But just as Seneca believed in the transforming power of reason, and the ability of individuals to take responsibility for their own actions and the state of their souls, he also believed that each decision counts, is vital to the destiny and well-being of the self, and carries with it the freedom to create either health or disease, contentment or dissatisfaction, anxiety or serenity.

It is in the struggle to control desire that we learn how to live a human life, and by doing so make spiritual progress. By progressing in this way we are able to transform our mind, soul and character.

What else, in fact, can you be doing but making yourself daily a better person, discarding some portion of error, and recognising that the faults you thought were due to circumstance are your own?

For there are shortcomings we attribute to times and places, but they're bound to follow us, no matter where we go.

Stoicism, an almost forgotten philosophy, still provides a method of dealing with life that can secure personal happiness and coherence in the midst of a confusing and distracting society. To the ancients, philosophy wasn't just an academic subject to be studied formally. It wasn't a process of thinking for its own sake, or of writing discourses to analyse and define concepts. Instead it was a recipe for living, a set of well-worked-out ideas and principles that had to be proved not in the mind but in daily experience.

All philosophies can be considered as attitudes to life, ways of looking at the world, and we each maintain our own individual attitude. But philosophy takes that individual attitude and puts it to the test, tries to examine it through discourse and experience, shakes it out and tries to discover if it successfully covers all of life, or if it is only makeshift opinion full of gaping holes.

This process was begun by Socrates in Athens in the fifth century BC. He made a practice of testing his fellow Athenians, all of whom had very strong attitudes and philosophies (even if they would never have used such an elevated term to describe them). Socrates' method was to ask the people of Athens questions until they realised that their answers were incomplete or that they contradicted themselves. He uncovered the holes in their safety blankets, and they didn't like it.

Socrates never wrote a word of philosophy, as far as we know. Instead, he lived it in the way he loved his family, looked after his friends and students, did his duty to the state, survived in a frugal and simple manner, and tried for much of his life to show his fellow citizens how to think about life.

Socrates never professed to teach virtue except by showing himself to be a virtuous man. He hoped by this means to make others virtuous. This was all he knew. He never claimed to have any real knowledge. He said:

As one man is pleased with improving his land, another with improving his house, so I am daily pleased in observing that I am growing better.

Socrates' example, and his shocking death by drinking poison, to which he was sentenced in 399 BC, led to a flowering of philosophy in Athens, and we can trace the Stoic trail that led from him to the cynics Diogenes and Crates, from them to their student Zeno, who founded

Stoicism, and then on a route via Panaetius, Posidonius and Cicero to Seneca, Epictetus and so on to Marcus Aurelius, the first philosopher-king and the last major Stoic.

Stoics v. Epicureans

Stoicism was the Romans' philosophy of choice. There were also believers, though fewer, in Epicureanism, and these two systems found themselves in conflict in Roman times. The simplest and crudest way to characterise the two is to say that Stoicism professed duty in the world and Epicureanism pleasure in seclusion, although both philosophies sought the same end result – the free enjoyment of an internal calm and contentment. The real difference between them is that Stoicism believed in a providential god, while Epicurus claimed the world was godless, a product of mere chance.

The poet Horace, the son of a freed slave, was an Epicurean, and his description of one of his typical days gives a good sense of an Epicurean life-style:

I wander wherever I fancy; ask the price of herbs and barley at the market; saunter sometimes around the Circus, that rendezvous of thieves and frauds, and sometimes around the forum in the dusk to listen to the fortune-tellers. Then I go home to a plate of leeks, pulse and rolls. Supper is served by three servants. On my marble side-table stand two cups, with a glass, and near them a coarse pitcher, a bottle and a small bowl, all homely Campanian ware. Then I go to sleep, uncon-

cerned about waking early in the morning.

I lie in bed till 10; then I get dressed, and either go out, or, having read or written something to amuse me, I go to the Campus Martius for exercise, where I'm massaged with oil. When I'm tired, and the scorching weather obliges me to bathe, I thereby avoid the intense heat. Having eaten a moderate lunch, not greater than will fill my stomach till the evening, I enjoy the rest of the day at home.

This is the life of those who are entirely free from the anxiety and uneasiness of the ambitious. I comfort myself with the idea that I shall live more happily amidst these pleasures than if my grandfather, uncle and father had all of them been high officials.

Horace wanted to enjoy simple pleasures and to avoid the 'anxiety and uneasiness' of Seneca's ambitious path. Personally, it wouldn't take me all that long to adapt to Horace's kind of life. All I would need, he says, is a small private income and a minimum of ten slaves. Richer men had more – one house in Rome had 400 slaves in attendance.

Horace shows us the ideal of Epicureanism: a life of quiet pleasure. Epicurus didn't consider riotous living, drunkenness and sensuality as the best kind of pleasure. He admitted they were productive of it, but he also said they produced annoying side-effects which outweighed the pleasure. For Epicurus the height of pleasure is simply the removal of pain. When pain is absent from both mind and body there is uninterrupted pleasure. And to live pleasantly is to live well, wisely and justly.

Stoicism wasn't in favour of a life of pleasure. The

Stoics didn't trust pleasure, because they saw how easily it becomes addictive and uncontrollable. Instead, they believed in a life of reason and virtue, one in which the only thing worth pursuing is good itself.

The Stoic Way

Stoicism was a kind of religion for its followers, which included many of the leading writers, thinkers and statesmen of the time. It was a religion without priests or a holy text, but it did have a creed of dogmas and a god. Its god, the *logos*, eventually infiltrated into Christianity as the 'Word', in the sense that the Gospel of John uses it:

In the beginning was the Word, and the Word was with God, and the Word was God.

For the Stoics the *logos* is a god of thought and speech, a god of reason who has providentially arranged the entire universe for good. This was a god who was also Fate and Nature, who expressed himself through Nature, and, by planting a divine spark of his own rationality in the soul of human beings, had given us the ability to reason, think and talk, and therefore to imitate the *logos* in our own lives. For reason, thought and speech represented the key to human life. As Socrates had said,

Haven't you realised, that whatever excellent principles we have learned by our civilisation, principles by which we know how to live, we learned only through the medium of speech?

Whatever valuable instruction any person acquires, he also acquires them by means of speech.

Don't those who teach best use speech? And those who know the most important truths are able to discuss them with the greatest eloquence?

Why else do I sit here in the market place every day talking to people like you and Plato and Simmias? Isn't it through speech that I try to communicate some knowledge and wisdom to you?

This idea of reason and speech as the divine creative force in human life goes back to the Hebrew Bible, back to God creating heaven and earth through speech:

And God said, 'Let there be light, and there was light.'

As Yahweh (God) explains to Moses in the Sinai desert,

'I will be there, and my Word will be your helper.'

I haven't brought Judaism in here gratuitously, but rather to explain what attracted the Greeks and Romans to the Stoic beliefs. For Stoicism fulfilled a need in Roman society that the old traditional religion could not satisfy.

The original Roman religion was a true pagan one. Based on earth and agriculture, it was tied purely to the land and the seasons and was an ethics-free zone. When the Romans came into contact with the superior culture of the Greeks, not only did they absorb much of Greek thinking, philosophy, art, history and poetry, they also incorporated their myths and gods. So Greek Zeus became Roman Jupiter, Herakles became Hercules and so on. Roman names were substituted for the Greek gods, who were introduced wholesale into Roman life.

But many educated Greeks and Romans had already discarded the gods as irrelevant, just as Epicurus taught that the gods did not exist. So Greeks and Romans were open to – in fact needed – a philosophy or a religion that could provide an ethical basis of life that fitted their new conditions – that of city dwellers in a growing and expanding civilisation.

Socrates' life and work can be seen as a one-man mission to provide a workable ethic for this new kind of life. He said when on trial for his life:

I shall go on saying, in my usual way, 'My friend, why do you, a citizen of the greatest and most famous city of the world for its wisdom, care so much about accumulating the greatest amount of money, glory and status, and so little of wisdom, truth and the improvement of your soul, which you never pay the slightest attention to? Aren't you ashamed of this?'

Because my only occupation is to go around persuading you all, young and old, to make your chief concern not your bodies or your possessions, but to care only for the most radical improvement of your souls. I will never stop telling you that wealth does not bring goodness, but instead it is from goodness that wealth and every other blessing comes both to the individual and to the state.'

Two hundred years after Socrates' failure, Zeno, the founder of Stoicism, began teaching a philosophy that combined physics, logic and ethics, and of these three ethics – the way a person behaves and acts towards others – was considered the most essential. Zeno tried to give, in a more systematic way than Socrates, an ethical basis to life, a positive code and method for conduct that could be taught, learned and acted upon. But where did Zeno's ethical teachings come from? Did he invent them himself or was he influenced by another source?

Zeno was a Phoenician from Cyprus, the son of a merchant who traded the famous purple-dyed cloth of the Lebanon to Athens and other Greek-speaking cities. The Phoenicians were a Semitic people, and their cultural claim to fame is that they devised the alphabet which we now use. Hundreds of years before, they had taught this alphabet to the Greeks, who had by themselves developed only an oral culture.

The Phoenicians were traders and sailors who set up colonies throughout the Mediterranean to sell their wares: wood, cloth, dye and metal objects. In the past they had also been trading partners with their neighbours, the Jews, who were closely allied to the Phoenicians by language, history and location. The Phoenicians had not only supplied the cedarwood for Solomon's Temple in Jerusalem, they also provided much of the skilled labour to build it.

As traders, the Phoenicians must have devised their alphabet for the purpose of accounting and record-keeping, because they have left us no written texts of a spiritual or ethical kind. My assumption, for which I cannot give any evidence, is that the ethics that Zeno had learned from his Greek–Phoenician background must have included Jewish ethics, the Laws of Moses.

We must remember that Stoicism was not an Athenian philosophy, even though Zeno studied in Athens. Almost all the leading Stoics of the Greek period, and even into Roman times, were Hellenistic Greeks from the Middle East and not from mainland Greece. They came from Rhodes, Tarsus, Soli, Babylon and other eastern parts of the ancient world.

Stoicism, like Judaism and Christianity, is a product of eastern thought. We only need recall that the Apostle Paul, the effective creator of Christianity, grew up as an assimilated Greek-speaking Jew in Tarsus, in Cilicia, one of the key centres of Stoicism. He would naturally, in that environment, have taken on both Jewish and Stoic beliefs, which eventually filtered through him into Christianity.

It is my belief that Jewish ethical teaching formed part of the basis for Zeno's thinking, and from the Roman Stoics flowed by a second route into Christian thought.

The Birth of the Individual

Stoicism was a 'New Age' philosophy for the third century BC. It differed from earlier philosophies in that it was designed as a way of life for individuals who had to become citizens of the world, at a time when the individual had only half emerged from the old clan or tribal matrix.

People were living increasingly in cities as opposed to the land, and this new kind of life presented unusual and original experiences and problems that the old traditions couldn't solve. Instead of being confined to the constant cycle of nature that agricultural life demands, the people of the cities became free-floating citizens who had to find new attitudes to a new style of life. And increasingly, they were forced to look beyond the narrow limits of their own city-state to the panoramic world outside.

This kind of change brings on fear and uneasiness. We are never prepared for the new, so every change becomes a test. We feel the need to cope and prove ourselves, and this requires great self-confidence. But the old self-confidence of the Romans and the Greeks had derived from the certainties of tribal life, the close instinctive responses of family and religion that dominated humanity's early social existence. This way of life was now unable to provide relevant answers to new events and structures in society.

Growing and prospering city-states, like Athens, Carthage and Rome, had great need for slaves and land, and they developed a maritime expansion of colonies and federations which took people out of their traditional family and tribal communities and placed them in a larger, looser and more alienating context.

This expanding world of commerce and politics was set in motion once men had ventured out from their own lands and voyaged to other societies, whether for trade or war, and discovered different ways of thinking about the world and relating to it. People were now forced to think for themselves, to discover how best to confront this larger world emerging around them.

The first person with the vision to attempt a universal expansion of power was Alexander the Great, who set his Greek armies marching as far east as India. Following his early death, all the states of his empire collapsed back into individual dynasties ruled by his various generals. The first expression of a universal empire was halted almost as soon as it began.

It was left to the Romans to conclude this expansion when they conquered the Carthaginians and Greeks and gained control of the entire Mediterranean basin. But their ideas, their attitude to life, their philosophy, were still too narrow to deal adequately with this change, and they needed to find a new way of looking at the world. Stoicism provided this.

According to Stoicism, each person not only belonged to his own community but was also a citizen of the world, a cosmopolitan. A local ruler might exercise control over his citizens' bodies and possessions, but Stoicism claimed that each person's ultimate authority was his or her own will. The Stoics' philosophy was an attempt to maintain freedom in the face of tyranny and this often brought them into conflict with local rulers.

Epictetus, a contemporary of Seneca, had been a slave of one of Nero's officers, and on being given his freedom became a Stoic philosopher. Because of his background, he knew what life was like around the court of Nero.

What is it that disturbs and terrifies people? Is it Caesar and his guards? I don't think so. It's not possible that the will which is by nature free can be disturbed by anything else, or obstructed by anything other than itself. But it is a person's own opinions which disturb him.

When Caesar threatens me, I say 'Who do you threaten?' If

he says, 'I will put you in chains,' I say, 'You threaten my hands and feet.' If he says, 'I will cut off your head,' I reply, 'You threaten my head.' If he says 'I will throw you in prison,' I say, 'You threaten the whole of my poor body.' If he threatens me with exile I say the same.

Doesn't he threaten me at all then? If I feel that all these things don't concern me, then he doesn't threaten me at all. But if I fear any of them, then it really is I whom he threatens. Who then do I fear? The master? Which master? The master of things which are in my own power? There is no such master. Then do I fear the master of things which are not in my power? But what do these things mean to me?

Caesar says, 'I intend to conquer your opinions as well.' Who has given him this power? How can you conquer the opinions of another person? 'I will conquer it by applying terror to it,' he says. Doesn't he know that opinion conquers itself, and isn't conquered by another? That nothing else can conquer the will but the will itself.

A Philosophy Of Freedom

When we look at the surface of human life, the multifarious and frenetic activities swirling around us, we're struck by a dizzying sequence of events seemingly occurring at random, all chance connections and mix-ups. All this frenetic turmoil and haphazard activity appears to be uncontrolled, and we assume we're unable to exert any personal control over it.

Instead we concentrate on controlling that part of life that we feel we can control: our own thoughts and activities. Following our need for self-survival, we use our mind and body in ways that we think will help us best to survive and prosper. We try to avoid those things we fear: poverty, ill-health, death.

The Stoics realised that one of the key problems to this approach is that people expend a great deal of their time and energy, both physical and mental, in trying to obtain possessions or goods that they may never actually acquire, or that they will subsequently lose. This failure to fulfil our desires and the frustration we feel in trying to hold on to things that are unpredictable and transient lead to those familiar feelings of unhappiness, anxiety and fear. We try so hard to avoid misfortunes that in the end appear to be inevitable. It's almost as if we bring on the things we fear the most.

The Stoics thought this problem could be avoided, and they worked out a method by which people would seek only those goods that it was possible and easy to obtain, and avoid those that caused the greatest problems. In this way feelings of frustration and anxiety would not arise. In their place would be a feeling of serenity and contentment.

The Stoics said that all our values depend on the judgements we make. Our mind is free to determine what is good and therefore worthy of pursuit, and what is bad and therefore to be avoided. By pursuing only the good the mind can find contentment and happiness, and by avoiding the bad can avoid all that anguish and fear. Everything depends on the way a person uses his or her mind to see and interpret the world.

Everyone's mind is free to make choices, and this ability to choose represents the fundamental freedom of the human spirit. We have a choice as to whether we want to pursue good or evil, right or wrong, but because these are relative concepts that depend on varying conditions of time, place and circumstance, it's not always easy to determine the right choice. The Stoics came up with a simple guideline, a handy rule to apply when making these decisions.

They said that in all the choices we make, we only need to be aware of two possibilities, and we can put these to ourselves in the form of a single question. Does the thing or object that I desire depend on my will or not? Because if it is something that depends on my will, then I can effect a real control over it, and it's good to pursue it. But if it's something that doesn't depend on my will, then I can't exert control over it and must let it pass. Because if we try to control things that we're unable to control, we will cause trouble for ourselves, will be disappointed and hurt.

Now, the list of things that the Stoics said we can control is extremely limited. They taught that the only thing we control is our own thoughts and our will, and nothing else. Our bodies, children, money, possessions and so on, all the things we normally believe we have control over, they believe we do not control.

For example, we think of 'our children', as if we have control over them. We may, for a short period, but once they get old enough to think and act independently, we soon lose that control.

We believe we control our own bodies, both consciously and unconsciously, but as we age or become ill, we realise that we have only limited, not absolute control. We may be able to prolong our lives through mental and physical practices like meditation and yoga, but in the end our bodies are subject to deterioration and decay. We have even less control over money and possessions, as Chance (or Fortune in Seneca's terms) dictates whether we acquire and hold on to things or not.

The Stoics believed that our will, which represents our freedom, should be involved only in making decisions about good and evil. These are the only two actions that we really have control over, that depend on us. Everything else – money, a person's body, reputation and so on – they called 'indifferent' or neutral, and they thought that our attitude to these indifferent things needed to be quite detached. So we shouldn't get worked up and disturbed in relation to these neutral things, because in the end we have no real control over them. We need just to accept them as part of nature and not the essential parts of us.

The Stoics were not otherworldly saints who ignored the reality of life. They understood that the things that are not under our control, that they called indifferent or neutral, are in fact the things that most people consider 'good', and sweat, agonize and fight over. We need money to live, and want a healthy body and loving relationships to enjoy our time on earth. The stoics agree that of the indifferent things some, like health and wealth, are more advantageous than others, like illness and poverty. But even though health and wealth are advantageous, it doesn't make sense to pursue them as goods or become disturbed by them, since it isn't up to us whether we become healthy or wealthy. These things do not rely on our will, but on chance, fate and nature. What's important is the well-being of our soul and this is dictated by the mental approach we take to the world in general.

What should really disturb us is if we make poor decisions about good and evil by failing to understand the difference between real and apparent good and evil, and therefore live a life of illusion or even delusion. If we seek for the good only in worldly goods and not in our souls, then our life may lead to pain and suffering, exactly what we want to avoid.

The Stoic attitude to life is an attentive and aware disposition towards the people, events and things with which we come into contact, so that we're able to deal properly with each of them. This Stoic attitude of attentiveness is very close to the Buddhist ideal of mindfulness. Both ask for the mind's awareness, an active consciousness, to be applied in all the moments of existence. And since we're fully aware in each moment of existence, we're able to respond immediately and properly to events.

Here is a famous example from recent history of someone making a poor choice by not asking that key question – does this person depend on my will or not? When former President Bill Clinton met Monica Lewinsky one fateful night at the White House, he wanted to make love to her. But by making a false judgement, by letting his desire have its head (so to speak) even though Monica was not under the control of his will, he brought a great deal of avoidable trouble on himself, on Monica, on his wife and on many of his supporters and friends.

Even though Monica may have desired Bill even more than he desired her, the fact that he was a married man, and not just the President, meant that he too could not be under her control. This relationship was doomed to cause suffering.

Stoicism is not against sex, although it recognises that the pleasure to be found in sensuality is both powerful and addictive and therefore has to be carefully considered. When people are free to make love, mutually desire it, and no one will be hurt or damaged by their love-making, there is no barrier to impulse. But adultery, though seductive and attractive, always leaves some damage behind.

A Stoic like Seneca expects that the pursuit of the good will carry its own reward. His expectation is that making good decisions for yourself and feeling positive about the actions you choose will make you feel good not only about yourself but also in yourself. This feeling is not just psychological but physiological as well, since doctors today understand that by acting in a straightforward, direct and honest way we are able to combat stress and foster good health. As Seneca said,

How much better it is to follow the straight path and make your way to a point at which you find satisfaction in realising a fine ideal. We succeed in this when we understand that there are two classes of things inviting or repelling us. We are invited by riches, pleasure, physical beauty, spectacle, and other things that beguile and please. We are repelled by exertion, death, pain, disgrace, and poverty. We must therefore train ourselves neither to dread the latter nor desire the former. Let us battle with them, retreating before the things that invite, and encountering with spirit those that attack.

Does happiness consist of anything more than feeling good about yourself?

3

The Sleeping Giant

Just as Stoicism provided the Graeco-Roman world with a new attitude, a philosophy, to cope with major structural changes in society, so we too need a revised philosophy of life to cope with twenty-first-century changes.

As in Imperial Rome, there is a moral breakdown in our society and things feel out of control, shifting and dangerous. Stability and certitude are hard to find, and we feel spiritually adrift. Traditional religions experience difficulty in offering answers to our spiritual problems, and one response to this failure has been a shift to the extreme position of fundamentalism. Those whom religion cannot reach take refuge in cynicism and nihilism, or search, like the ancient Romans who found ecstatic release in eastern cults, for healing ideas and values in eastern religions.

But unlike the Romans, we are suffering from a change in Nature itself. Climatic change, which appears to be the cause of damaging alterations in weather patterns, has brought uncontrollable flooding, fires and drought to all parts of the globe. This is a long-term trend with fearsome implications for everyone, yet governments enthralled by economic growth are unwilling to confront the problem. No one in power is willing to do anything that will upset the status quo, and so we drift in a political vacuum, waiting for nature to supply her own remedy, one that is likely to be drastic.

The Romans never developed an advanced science or technology because slaves were their living labour-saving devices. But scientific knowledge and technology are at the heart of our society's growth, and scientists have now succeeded in the incredible feat of breaking the genetic code. Through this knowledge we have the ability to create life through cloning, and this has thrown up new challenges to the moral order.

As in the Graeco-Roman world, new questions have arisen that require new thinking. What is life? Can life be patented? Does it have an intrinsic value, or merely a dollar value? What attitude should we take to these new developments? What opinion do we have about their meaning? Do we allow science to develop everything that is technically possible, or do we impose decisions about what is acceptable and what is not? These questions, and others like them, demonstrate ethics in action, and show that philosophy has a role to play in contemporary life. It can give us the tools to clarify these problems, and decide what kind of life it is we want to lead.

To understand these fundamental and complex questions we need concerned and aware citizens able to use their minds to the full: rational, emotional and imaginative. But our society, like Roman society, does not encourage this kind of citizen. Rome used to keep its poor urban population quiet with free bread and gladiatorial games, and we have substituted for these ancient palliatives drugs and television, hoping that the anger and frustration of those at the bottom of our economic heap can be kept pacified and under control, while those at the top get on with business as usual. Marx was wrong about religion being the opium of the people; opium has turned out to be the opium of the people.

The Global Village

The worldwide empire that Alexander the Great dreamed of, that the Romans finally created and developed, that Napoleon and all the European empire-builders of the nineteenth century emulated, has now reached a new stage of progress. This is the global economy promoted by the World Trade Organisation, but it doesn't represent an empire controlled by one nation, but rather an empire controlled by a philosophy – that of the free market in goods and services.

We live in a globally connected world with an economic structure that systematically transfers wealth from some parts of the world to other parts. In Rome wealth was transferred from the distant provinces to the aristocrats in the capital. In our times wealth is transferred from the poor to the rich, from the undeveloped countries to the developed. This transfer isn't entirely the workings of chance or accident, but is partly deliberate and planned.

By our silent consent, through an economic and political system – a philosophy which we do not try to change because we are among its beneficiaries – we are helping to destroy people the Stoics tell us are our brothers and sisters. People in the developing world – from Uganda to Iraq and Bangladesh to South Africa – are subject to disease, hunger and death so that many of us are able to live an increasingly affluent and wasteful life-style.

The media have little interest in explaining the interconnections between our wealth and Third World poverty, the link between our economic system and the destruction of the earth. But these connections are real and they result from a philosophy that we live by. The power of this philosophy is shown in its effects on the people who are not benefiting from it. For these people, the victims, it is not a philosophy of life but one of fear, pain, suffering and death.

Greed Is Good

Every economic or political system has a philosophy behind it, even if that philosophy is never explicitly stated. The philosophy of the global society that is now developing is one that contains the core American values of 'life, liberty and the pursuit of happiness'. Globalisation of the economy, the creation of the global village, is an attempt to export this philosophy to all the peoples of the world.

In theory, 'life, liberty and the pursuit of happiness' are excellent values, but in practice this philosophy equates happiness exclusively with acquiring money, and it demands that everyone living under it compete fiercely with each other for material goods. It's a philosophy of winners and losers, and it dictates that we all strive to be winners and fear becoming losers. To become a winner, to succeed in this race of life, we need to develop a strong ambition.

We have seen the results of Seneca's ambition 2,000 years ago. His story shows us that, as the Stoics predicted, the 'indifferent' things that he desired, and over which his will had no real control, brought him mainly trouble and unhappiness. Seemingly innocent events led to disastrous consequences. Seneca's life, besides illustrating the Stoic truism that wealth doesn't bring happiness, shows us how difficult it is to combine activity in the world with an ethical life.

We are impelled to make money to live, and the ethos of our time is, the more the better. We pursue money initially to secure our survival, but it is extremely rare for us to stop at the stage of sufficiency. We go on to seek more and more money, spending it to maintain status with our peers – all of this to ensure that we see ourselves, and are seen by others, as a success.

But we never stop to ask what all this success is ultimately for. Why do we want all this money and all these possessions? What does success give us, that we expend so much of our life in pursuit of it? Do we have to behave in this way? If so, then where, in this world, can we find peace? In such a world, where do we go for guidance?

Many people look to the famous, the top people in society, to see how they are acting. These role models are often literally just that – models and film stars – but they have quite possibly less idea of what to do than ordinary people.

We are obsessed with the exploits of these contemporary icons in magazines and on television, and look on them with envy because of their wealth and fame. They have everything that we have been told will lead to the good life – beauty, money, fame, power, status, leisure – yet their divorces, drug and sexual habits, and eccentric tastes for spiritual enlightenment (as well as diet) show that they're just as lost as the rest of us.

We are subject from an early age to mass media infiltration and educational training that give us few tools with which to build up a strong sense of personal self. Our sense of self is weak and we're left confused and uncertain about who we are, and what our role in life is. What we need is to shore up that immature and tentative self, to find out just who we are and what we believe. Until we can do this, we will not be able to change ourselves or anything else in our world, but will merely drift with the tide of received opinion. And this opinion is manipulated by people who would prefer that we do not think for ourselves.

Our immature, uncultivated self is unable to cope with ageing, death and illness. To cease being young is the great curse of our times. We desire to live up to a surface beauty, an image that advertising and the media propose to us as the ideal of human life. We have lost the confidence that our own self contains greater value than the manufactured and marketed self with which the media bombard us. Are we still capable of understanding what Socrates meant when he said,

If your will is beautiful, then you will be beautiful.

Have we lost both the tools and the desire to discover who we really are?

This inability to discover and accept our own self and the bodies we have been given often leads to early feelings of low self-esteem. In those who don't have the 'right' shape and size it can lead to intense self-loathing. People turn to plastic surgery to change who they are on the outside, while remaining the same on the inside. Few are willing to change the minds they have been given, to realise that just as bodies can be altered and changed through surgery, so the mind can also be altered, in both good and bad ways. Religious cults and fundamentalism show us how damaging some mind-altering ideologies can be, but transforming movements like Buddhism and Taoism show us healthy and positive alternatives.

Like Buddhism, Seneca's philosophy provides a way to think for yourself and to strengthen that inner core. Seneca wrote to show his contemporaries how it was possible to maintain coherence of mind, body and soul in the midst of a seemingly incoherent world. To Seneca human freedom is found in the will, in our ability to make decisions. For many of us, living a life of illusion, we expect freedom to be found in money.

The Fall of Empires

The new globalisation, with its desire for continuous growth, is ignoring the limitations placed on that growth by the world itself. If a billion Chinese and a billion Indians try to duplicate the suburban American way of consumption and acquisition, then the resources of the earth will be quickly degraded and finally depleted in the process. Further global warming and extreme climatic change will take place, and we will find ourselves living in an increasingly unstable, unhealthy, violent and dangerous world.

What the world needs is a sustainable economy, and in a strange way this means a Stoic economy, in the sense that we need to understand the limitations imposed on us by the world in order to discover a way of life that fits comfortably within those limitations.

The fall of the Roman Empire shows us that even the mightiest of global powers can topple from a collective inability to solve internal structural problems. In the face of that failure we need to take seriously the environmental problems facing us in this new century, and to find the political will to make the changes we need, changes that the Romans failed to make. In Seneca's words:

Why, all, all those cities of whose magnificence and renown you now hear – time will sweep away their very traces. There have been glorious cities in Achaia: see how their very foundations have perished utterly, till nothing is left to witness their bare existence. It's not only things made with hands that decay, nor only structures raised by human skill and industry that the ages overturn: mountains crumble away, whole districts have been known to subside; landmarks once far out of sight of the sea now lie beneath its waters. The fury of volcanic fires has sapped the hills on which they once gleamed, and levelled what once were soaring peaks, the mariner's beacon and comfort. Yes, even the works of nature herself suffer: then mustn't we contemplate the downfall of cities with resignation? Fall they will!

One thing I know, and it's this: all the works of mortal hand lie under sentence of mortality: we live among things doomed.

Can we change our way of living, or are we doomed to repeat the lessons of history? Life doesn't stand still, everything changes, and even human nature alters. Perhaps hope is to be found in the new relationship that has developed between men and women over the last thirty years. With women at last taking a greater role in society, we may yet see new and healthier attitudes emerging towards human ambition, desire and the ever-creative human spirit.

Humanitas

We have inherited, through writers like Seneca and Cicero, the Roman concept of *humanitas*, which has given us an image and example of a humane and just society. This inheritance may ultimately be the true and abiding legacy of Rome.

For cultivated and educated Romans *humanitas* implied an open, curious, fair, kindly, intelligent and witty approach to life. They took many of their ideas from the Greek stoics, including the belief in the common bond of all humanity, a belief which led to the concept of the equality of all people. Roman jurists influenced by these Stoic ideas changed Roman law from a system based on society's need for order to one based on the human desire for justice. This legacy of the rule of law tempered by mercy and justice has given us the potential to create a world where social justice is not just an empty platitude but one that can become a living reality.

In Seneca's time, and in later European history, the style of mind represented by *humanitas* could be lived only by an aristocratic élite, cushioned by inherited wealth that gave them freedom from necessity and the leisure time to read, think and explore the world. In Roman and Victorian times, *humanitas* found a home among people living in country houses, with private libraries, and opportunities to gather and discuss ideas. But the essence of *humanitas* is a quality of mind, an appreciation of culture and education, and a desire to foster civilisation.

During the past 100 years, new social conditions have developed that require middle- and working-class children to spend fifteen to twenty years of development in full-time education. Life-long learning has become a necessity for a society undergoing continuous and dramatic change.

Conditions now exist enabling the children and grandchildren of poorly educated, semi-literate and even illiterate families to acquire an attitude to life similar to *humanitas*, which not very long ago was only available to a rich and privileged minority élite. This patrician attitude in western society has traditionally been deeply conservative and when challenged by social and class change has turned repressive. It was a philosophy protective of the interests of the dominating class in society. But economic power and dominance has moved away from small numbers of land- and factory-owning élites and has filtered down to a larger mass of intellectual workers, people who work with their minds rather than with their bodies.

The children of these workers, who unlike earlier generations are raised in comfortable homes that place a value, sometimes the highest value, on culture and education, are privileged to have enough leisure for the long years of schooling, training and higher education demanded by the new economy. Whether they will seize this opportunity or waste it is yet to be seen, but there is no doubt that the democratisation of *humanitas* has radically changed the dynamics of society.

The Power of the Word

One hundred years ago my grandparents left a repressive regime in Poland and Russia to start a new life in America. They left behind them a traditional village life, where the future promised only a worsening of existence: religious pogroms, oppression and war. Although they could read and write, their knowledge was limited by a narrow religious upbringing in a rural setting.

Their children, my parents, born and raised in the New World, had no opportunity to acquire an education. They had to leave school at ages nine and thirteen to find jobs to help support their large families. Growing to maturity during the great economic depression of 1929, they never had the time or the money to pursue a higher culture. But many of their children, the grandchildren of immigrants, have been able to pursue higher education, have had the benefit of money and leisure to travel, and the time and freedom to read and think. This book itself can be seen as the result of such a social and cultural evolution.

My immigrant grandparents were powerless, my uneducated parents were equally powerless, but I am powerful, not because I manipulate any force or have personal status or influence, but simply because I wield words – information. You, who have the time and leisure to read this book, are equally powerful, not because you are physically strong and aggressive, but because of a shift in society's resources. Your information, the product of your mind, holds the possibility of political power that potentially could transform not only your own life but the lives of those around you. It is your choice as to how you use your inherent power and knowledge, but it's important to realise that the power actually exists.

What has changed is the notion of power. In Rome power was always backed up by armed force, the ultimate coercion. However, in our time information has become an effective form of power, and Francis Bacon's maxim, 'Knowledge is power', has turned out to prophesy a transformation of society.

Knowledge and information have worldwide economic power and in our time seem to have surpassed armed aggression. It may be that conscious knowledge has now become a greater and more influential resource than instinctual and structured aggression.

This advance in society to an information age gives an advantage to those who are information creators, carriers or providers, those who work with their minds more than their muscles, and they are now the dominant class in society. Not only are they wealth creators but they are able to retain enough of the resources they create to become relatively prosperous themselves. This new class of wealthy, educated and influential workers represents a 'sleeping giant'.

The giant sleeps because, unaware that things have changed, it is not conscious of how much power it actually has. This power is intellectual in the authorship of e-mails, letters and articles, political both in the sense of votes at election time and the ability to protest and demonstrate physically, and, most important of all, economically in the form of purchasing power. The ability to decide which products to buy, which to stop buying, and which companies to support or boycott are all-powerful weapons in a mass consumer market.

It is rare for this giant to stir, but when it does, as in the misguided attempt to introduce genetically modified foods into the UK, then the government and the multinational corporations standing behind it are unable to budge and manipulate this creature, but must give way before it. The last fifty years have seen the growing political influence and power of the giant corporations that control so much of the world's wealth and resources. Because these corporations work together in pressure groups, and have finance available to fund election campaigns, they have managed to usurp power over governments, replacing the position of the electorate.

The twenty-first century may well see a global battle between the new educated élite and the giant multinationals. Once this sleeping giant awakes and becomes enlightened, there is no limit to what it can do. Its new communication system, the internet, gives it the ability to have instant global responses to events.

No Regrets

A few years ago, at the Cannes Film Festival, I had a drink with an old friend who had recently sold his film company for a large sum of money and had personally received many millions for his shares. Having worked hard at his business for thirty years he should have been able to relax and take life more easily, handing over the details to younger employees. But he didn't seem to be taking to semi-retirement, and instead wanted to be back in the thick of the action where he had been for so many years.

He asked me how old I was, and I told him that in a few months I would be fifty-five. He informed me that fifty-five was called the 'double nickel' and it was the age that signalled to men that any dreams still unrealised were destined never to come to fruition. From this age on regret was inevitable.

I realised that my friend, who was still a few years from the double nickel, was already feeling these regrets, and his unhappiness, even with a fortune in the bank, was all too palpable. I felt sorry for him, sorry that for all his striving and fighting for so many years to achieve his ambition – wealth, influence, status and power – he was not satisfied with what he had acquired and still had regrets for all the unfulfilled yearning that inhabited his soul.

But he was right. I did have many youthful dreams that were never going to be fulfilled. However, if I thought clearly about it, the dreams that remained unrealised could be numbered in the thousands. Among countless others, I was never going to ride through Paris in a convertible blue Bentley, own a Learjet, ride ponies on my own ranch, or preside, as my friend did, over a business empire.

If I had brooded over the things I hadn't achieved or accomplished by the time I was fifty-five, I could have made myself miserable, rehearsing in my mind all the bad decisions that had left me bereft of the glowing achievements that I had coveted as a young man. This useless anguish would have poisoned my remaining years, leaving me the kind of sour old man that I sometimes encounter: angry with their children, angry with their lives, angry at old age and impending death, angry at the world.

Instead, I realised it was the odd surprises, the unplanned and unexpected people and things that came my way that filled (and continue to fill) my life with pleasure and happiness. Ordinary day-to-day living, raising children, working and sharing with others, finding pleasure in the simple facts of life and nature – these mundane things turn out to be the real prizes of life.

They may not have the surface glitter and sparkle of the flashy images from television and magazines that seduce us into craving more and more. Instead they glow as it were from within, and give off a radiance that, once you have learned to see and feel it, attracts the spirit to a relationship that is life enhancing and not deadening. It's so very sad that many of us miss these wonderful and magical times while wasting lives worrying about the inessential. As the saying goes, 'Life is what happens while you're making plans.'

Philosophy can help us to discover the important things of life by giving us a fresh way of looking at the world, and of living in it. It can help us remove anguish and bitterness and provide us with the possibility of finding a serenity better equipped for living, ageing and dying. My friend's attitude is characterised by the T-shirt popular in the 1980s: 'Life's a race to own the most things, and then you die.' If this is all life is, then we all might as well die now, because this is not living, only existing and acquiring.

We are in danger of losing the true self, and need to relearn an art of living and wisdom. Stoicism, in the form of Seneca's thoughts and principles, shows us one way to live a life of values, and such a life can provide guidance and consolation in a world gone mad. Seneca himself looked forward to a time when his compromised life, despised both in his own time and by later scholars, could be vindicated:

Virtue is never lost to sight. There will come a time when she will be revealed, though she was hidden away or suppressed by the spite of her contemporaries. Someone who thinks only about his own generation is born merely for the few. But thousands of years and millions of people will come after you, and your concern should be with them.

Malice may have imposed silence on the mouths of those who were alive in your day. But there will arise people who will judge you without prejudice and without favour. If there is any reward that virtue receives at the hands of fame, not even this can pass away. Indeed, we ourselves shall not be affected by the talk of posterity.

Nevertheless, posterity will cherish and celebrate us even though we will not be conscious of it.

MARK FORSTATER
QUEENS PARK, LONDON, APRIL 2001

PART TWO

To Live's No Dainty Business

Victoria Radin

1

A Kind of Song

I'm writing for the generations of the future. I'm setting down some thoughts I hope will be useful to them, remedies whose effectiveness I've tested on my own wounds, which may not be cured, but at least have stopped bleeding. I'm guiding others to the right path, which I've discovered only late in life, when I am tired of wandering.

❖ Before all else, learn how to feel joy.
❖ Hurry to live. And measure a life in each day.
❖ Seek the health of your soul. Where does that lie? In not finding your pleasures in deceptions.
❖ It takes the whole of a life to learn how to live.

A warning
Accept life on the same terms as the weather. Things will come at you and sometimes they will hit you. Living is no dainty business. You've begun on a long road – you will have stumbles and twists and falls, and get tired and wish – or pretend to! – for death.

At one point you will leave a companion; at another you will bury one; at still another you will find an enemy.

These are the sorts of things you'll encounter all along the way. You can't escape the terms of life, but you can resist them.

A rule

Cling for all you're worth to the following: never give in to adversity; don't you dare trust prosperity; and always remember that the throw of the dice will happen as it will, without your requests. The blow you've anticipated will do the least harm.

A prayer

This should be your prayer. Let me die knowing that I behaved honourably, and that no one's freedom was lessened by my actions – least of all my own.

A question

How can the mind find a smooth and steady course, which does itself good? How can it find a balance, and sail along without ups and downs? In short, how can it find tranquillity?

A command

Be the sculptor of your own life.

2

The Soul Doctor

Seneca tries the talking cure with a troubled young friend who lived 2,000 years age, but whom you'll recognise.

TROUBLED YOUNG FRIEND:
I find myself languishing in an in-between state – I'm not sick but I'm not well. I have to admit to you that I'm irritable and quick to take things the wrong way. Worse, I'm getting used to it: I've begun to love my faults as much as my better points. For example, I insist that I'm perfectly happy being careful with money, and am not tempted by beautiful, expensive things. Then – wham! I go to an elegant dinner at a wealthy home and all my resolutions expire in the flambé. I find myself wondering: is my way of living *really* better? Or am I just fooling myself?

At the first sign of something which makes me feel I'm not coping, or that I've let myself down, I give up and want to crawl home and hide.

All this navel-gazing has done nothing but make me see myself through an even denser fog. Am I simply suffering from a failure of good intentions? How many people can be truthful with themselves? Who isn't always, secretly, their own biggest fan? I'm talking to you as if you were a doctor: please tell me if there's a cure for all this self-destructive dithering.

SENECA'S REPLY:
I shall continue your medical analogy for – if I may be a little pompous – we philosophers like to think of ourselves as physicians of the soul. You're like someone who's just recovered from a serious illness. You're cured, but unused to being healthy. You're still worried and distraught, imagining symptoms that no longer exist. Your ailment isn't a storm but a sort of sea-sickness.

What you're really longing for is the greatest good available to us – that of stability. The Greeks called this state of mind 'well-being of the soul'. I call it tranquillity, or peace of mind. I want to help you find it by restoring your confidence in yourself.

The fact that you admit you're in trouble is half the battle. Think how much more you'd dislike yourself if you were entangled in lies and self-deceptions. This is true of most people, and they're the ones who are ill with self-hatred.

Now let's have a look at all the splendid possibilities for havering and vacillating and punishing yourself.

Some people spin around like insomniacs, changing their minds every other minute, constantly deciding to do the thing they had just decided not to do. Only utter exhaustion brings them to rest.

Others are afflicted with boredom and to evade it constantly change their goals.

Other people suffer from inertia, and can't find the

will to live as they would like. Instead they remain stranded where they began.

Still others are totally in the clouds.

And others constantly yearn for the past.

The malady I'm describing in these different forms is one disease – dissatisfaction with yourself.

These are the results:

If you're indecisive, you live perpetually in a state of suspense. You'll find yourself doing things that you know are wrong for you. You'll become afraid of attempting anything that really matters.

You can't control your desires, and you can't fulfil them. Here's a soul stewing in its half-abandoned hopes.

You may try to run away from life: but the paradox is that you've crashed into this state through lack of inner resources, and this failure is what hits you when you've slunk off on your own. You've said goodbye to the pleasures of company and going out. But staying home is intolerable and isolating.

You feel shamed by your predicament, with unfortunate results: you become more and more inward, dithering and mourning and envious of what you see as the good luck of others. To speak medically again, the symptoms become like an itch that needs to be scratched, and you learn to expect and even enjoy aggravation.

In this state it's hardly surprising that you are literally sick of yourself. You think that by escaping your home, family or country you can get away from yourself as well and so you travel: 'Let's go to Rome!' That having failed, it's on to a camping trip – the country now, the city later. As another philosopher, Lucretius, said:

'Everyone flees himself.' But of course the reverse happens. You dog yourself, your most tedious and least loving companion.

So, my young friend, there you have it! I shall give you the prescription for preserving your peace of mind, for restoring it, and for building immunity to the faults that can take you by surprise.

First of All, Think Yourself Rich or Poor

A True Story

My teacher used to tell this tale:

'For a long time I was in love with expensive things. A gleam here, a gorgeous shape there, a lovely scent – and I'd be overcome. I naïvely assumed that the inside was as thrilling as the outside.

'One day I happened to come across a pageant of Rome's treasures – statues carved in gold and silver, elaborate jewellery, lush embroidered tapestries, platoons of elegantly costumed, good-looking boys and girls drilled to perfection, and all the other exhibitions of seeming greatness that an imperial power loves to put on show.

'I reviewed the spectacle and asked myself: 'What does this really do for people but inflame their sense of greed and envy? What does this parade of cash really mean? Have we assembled here for a lesson in how to covet material goods?

'Yet in fact I went away less tempted than before. I've learned to despise riches not only because they're unnecessary, but because they're insignificant. In a few short hours the procession had passed. Here was something that couldn't fill even a day. Yet it fills the whole of life for us.'

How blind and arrogant we are!
The money and status to content us doesn't exist. The folly of it! Creatures are destined to die – dying every day in fact – and nothing is enough for us.

Imagine this…
Suppose all the loot of all the world's big money-grubbers fell into your lap, and you became richer than any single person has ever been, living in houses all over the world fitted with all the latest gadgets as well as roofs of gold and floors of priceless mosaics made of the most precious gems, so that you not merely own but walk on treasures. Throw in paintings, sculptures, your own orchestra, composer and singers, your private theatre troupe and dramatist to perform in your own sumptuous auditorium, clothes that would make a peacock blush, more servants than there are populations of countries, and teams of therapists and advisers. Do you know what? All these things, every whim satisfied and catered for, will only induce in you the lust for more and more. Natural desires are limited – but those that arise from the artificial, from other people's ideas of what is good, are endless: for there is no point at which they can be satisfied. There will always be something else to crave.

*Here's how to become rich: a short cut to becoming a
billionaire*
I'm sure you're avid to know! Even with a short cut,
you'll still need funds: raise a loan, but not from the
bank. Borrow from yourself. However small the loan is,
it will be enough – and if there's a shortfall you can apply
to yourself for more. The secret is that there's no difference between having things and not wanting them.

*You can't always get what you want, but if you try, you can
get what you need or enough really is enough.*

- ❖ Those of us who are on good terms with poverty can
  count ourselves rich.
- ❖ Without the concept of thrift, no amount of money is
  ever enough.
- ❖ The person who is truly impoverished is not the one
  who has little but the one who yearns after more.
- ❖ It's for the unnecessary things that we sweat and
  slave and scour the world.

Enjoy feeling satisfied.

- ❖ If you want to make yourself rich, instead of multi-
  plying your wealth, subtract from your desires.
- ❖ None of us can have everything we want. But we can
  desist from wanting what we don't have.
- ❖ Nature requires that the belly be filled – not flattered.
- ❖ Likewise, Nature's only wish is that our thirst should
  be healthily quenched. Whether the glass is the finest
  crystal makes no difference.

Pride should have nothing to do with your bank account.

❖ We don't extol poverty in itself. But we do praise the person whom poverty leaves undefeated.

❖ There's a bigness of spirit in those who can retain the spirit of poverty in the midst of wealth.

The worry of having money makes us forget the point of it.

❖ To enjoy having wealth you had better not make yourself its servant.

❖ We often say: He's down with a fever. We could just as easily affirm: He's down with greed.

❖ It would be wonderful if before you pray for wealth, you observe what it is really like to possess it.

❖ The lives of those who work hard to gain what they then must work harder to keep are anxious and small.

❖ For the wealthy, everything they fail to own is a loss.

❖ The newly rich think everything depends on their wealth. Thus they forget themselves and become a little mad.

Wealth can't cure the mind of its maladies.

❖ If poverty upsets us, wealth will have the same result.

❖ It makes no difference whether you put sick people on a bed made of gold or of wood. Move them where you can, they'll take their illness with them.

❖ Riches are not where we pile them up. It is the soul, not the safe, that we need to fill.

What you have is only on loan.

❖ *The story of one loan*
When the philosopher Zeno was told of a shipwreck in which all his possessions had been lost to the sea, he said: 'Now I shall be able to follow my philosophy with fewer impediments.'

❖ *The story of another loan*
'But I'm being turfed off the land owned by my father and my grandfather!' you tell me. Tell me something else. Who was the owner before your grandfather? Can you name the family, or the individual, whose it was originally? You can only be a tenant. Whose tenant? Your heir's, and then only if you're fortunate.

❖ We should hold ready the gifts that have been granted to us and when called on to do so, give them back without complaining.
❖ Use your money happily instead of boasting about it. But use it sparingly, remembering that it is only a deposit.
❖ The person who ignores reason in their tenure of wealth has never retained it for very long.

Society, however disunited on other issues, is unanimous on the subject of greed — it wallows in it. People look up to money, they pray for it for themselves and for those they love. They offer it up as if it were the noblest possession they could possibly have.

Greed has a low I.Q.

- ❖ Most of the things we're desperate to own, for which we move mountains, on inspection prove either useless or actually damaging.
- ❖ We're ready to acquire things at the price of anxiety, danger, freedom and time, throwing away our self-respect in the process, things we wouldn't exchange a chair for. The truth is that there's nothing a person holds more cheaply than themselves.
- ❖ What you have seized by dubious means, someone else may even more easily take from you.
- ❖ Don't wish for what you don't have. You may find yourself strenuously toiling for something that if it were offered to you, you would refuse.

In our lust for personal possessions we lose a more valuable universal good – that of our common humanity.

Another Little Story

His head was turned by gross wealth. This can be a failing of an individual or of an era. How he changed after he got rich! First, it was devotion to his person – his clothes, the gym, expensive hair and so forth; then the beguiling pornography of real estate; finally furnishings, or more specifically interior decorators. After everything was glowing with gold and steel and sleek with leather, the table was laid with unusual and bizarre dishes, for now he had the power to over-ride custom and indulge in a passionate affair with novelty. He ended by despising all that is ordinary and natural. But everything we need and are made of is natural and ordinary.

4

Truth, Lies and Gladiators: How to Keep Your Head When All About You are Having Theirs Hacked Off

For some reason I took myself off the other day to a gladiator show. Not, you may believe, with the intention of watching mud-smeared men in armour stab one another, but in the hope of enjoying one of the lunchtime interludes of mimes, jugglers and dancers, which are often witty and amusing.

But even by going out for the non-violent entertainment, I was rebelling against one of the rules I've made for myself, which is to avoid crowds of people. I find I never return home with quite the same set of moral values, nor the same settled sense of peace that I've worked so hard to achieve. In fact, I go home not only crueller and less civilised for having spent time among throngs of humanity, but also more snobbish, more self-indulgent and greedier.

Perhaps I was being punished for my foolhardiness by the fact that I found no pleasing intermezzo of charming mimes, jugglers, etc. Instead, there was a new kind of combat which made all previous ones look like foreplay. Forget that these people are human! Let's have butchery in its primal form!

These contestants wear no helmet or shield and have nothing to protect them from the blades of their opponents. Goodbye, swordsmanship and finesse! Let's just get quickly to the kill!

In the morning, these wretched people are thrown to bears and lions. At noon, their adversaries are spectators who volunteer for the task. The winner – O happy fellow! – is held over for another demonstration of man's contempt for man: death is the sole exit. This is the replacement for the delightful intermezzo.

I hear you say: 'You know these men were murderers themselves, or highwaymen.' But who deserves *this*? And what crime have we committed who watch it? Stab! Maim! Why does this man hold back from killing? And why doesn't that one die a more satisfying death?

And now there is an interval – which is: let's cut a few throats just to keep up the pace!

Can't anyone see that bad examples wreak havoc on those who witness them? All we can do is give thanks that this lesson in cruelty falls sometimes on deaf ears. We can make up our own minds about what the multitude deems magnificent spectacle, fit for the gods.

As much as I admire the judgement of great men, I would follow my own.

Learn to despise the pleasure that comes from feeling that you think with the majority.

- ❖ The mob is the worst exponent of the truth.
- ❖ Instead of being guided by reason, we're seduced by imitation.
- ❖ There are acts we wouldn't choose to perform, but when they're done by many people, we follow behind like sheep – as if a certain kind of behaviour had become worthwhile merely because it had become commonplace.
- ❖ There's no possibility of clear-sightedness for those who rely on that least truthful of guides, public opinion.
- ❖ The opinion of the majority is often the worst way of doing things. Just look at the people we appoint to govern us!
- ❖ The most obvious path is delusive. Live by copying others and you will betray yourself.

A cavil to the above and a conflict: You should neither become like the bad because they are many, nor be an enemy of the many because they are unlike you.

Who dares tell themselves the truth?

How deplorable are the things we admire! How much we resemble children who see in any torn shred of grime a treasure, who think more of that than of mother, father, sister or brother.

- ❖ All truth belongs to me.
- ❖ The true things go on unchanged. The false can't survive as they are.

❖ In falsehood there's no consistency – only flux and disagreement.

❖ Consider not only the truth of what you say; but whether the person you're speaking to can tolerate the truth.

❖ It's better to offend with the truth than to please with flattery.

Lies are gossamer-thin. If you look very hard, you can see the light shining through them.

Things are usually not as described.

❖ Wisdom is solid and steady and beautiful not on its surface but inside itself. It must be searched for. It is near, but you must look for it.

❖ We should measure things not by appearance but by function.

Talk, talk, talk.

❖ Bookish conversations, clevernesses, scholarly speeches and lines cribbed from philosophers don't demonstrate spiritual strength. Even the most cowardly person can do well in words. The good we have lies within us without advertisement.

And looking...

❖ We allow our eyes to deceive us. If we coat a ceiling in gold we create a lie, for under that goldleaf is rotting wood. And it's not only our houses that wear masks. Do you think everyone who laughs feels joy?

This was not cribbed from Shakespeare. (In fact it was the other way round.)

We mount the stage to play role after role and – our deepest disgrace – we are never ourselves. It is a splendid achievement to play only one part. Very few of us are capable of this: most of us are circus quick-change artists.

We take our cue from envy: faults are catching.

❖ A single example of profligacy or greed harms us. An acquaintance who leads a pampered life makes us weak and flabby-willed. A rich neighbour compels us to yearn for finery. Even an innocent and generous person will find that the malice of a companion has left some dust.

❖ You will still feel envy even when you are envied.

❖ Do you envy those people who appear to stand higher than you? Those heights are also precipices.

Pretensions and fashions.

❖ Let us renounce the desire for dining off gold dinner plates – but also refrain from thinking that cheap, ugly crockery is the hallmark of honest living.

❖ We should try to lead a life that may be more thoughtful than that of most people, but is not repugnant to them.

- ❖ It is far better to be scorned for your lack of glamour than to be tortured by continuous pretence.
- ❖ There is a difference between living modestly and living carelessly.

Roman bohemians: a caution.

Don't ape those self-declared non-conformists who are more concerned with flaunting themselves than with their souls. Discard a strangely retro style of dress, hair which could provide a nest for birds, a war with cutlery, and everything else that thinks eccentricity for its own sake is the dictionary definition of impressive.

Those of us who have brains are unpopular enough without these extravagances. What will happen if we make a drama from it?

No one on earth will keep what they hear to themselves.

Talk has an intoxicating charm which winkles out secrets as easily as love or alcohol. The problem is: no one can prevent themselves from repeating things. And nobody will repeat exactly what they hear. And having failed to keep the story to themselves, the name of the teller is the next revelation.

Everybody has someone to whom they confide all the gossip. Try as they can to keep silent, they will eventually breed a swarm of listeners. Thus, something that was a secret just a short time ago quickly transmogrifies into distorted common knowledge.

Reputations: those of today are not tomorrow's.

❖ Your conscience will be by your side, shaking its finger, long after the crowd has passed by.

❖ The person who thinks they belong only to their own generation was put on earth for just a small number of people. Many generations and millennia will follow. These are where you should direct your thoughts.

❖ Honour can be recognised without remarking on it. It's complete not only when it's greeted by silence, but when it' s booed by dissent.

A parable.

Fame is the shadow of goodness and will stalk goodness whether goodness wants its company or not. But just as shadows sometimes precede, follow or walk alongside you, so fame sometimes goes ahead of us, in full display to everybody, and sometimes trails behind – even larger for arriving late, after envy has said goodbye. We needn't shout about our efforts. They will be known.

5

Living Now:
Make Every Day a
Whole Life

A Story of Time Regained:
Can This Ancient Person Really Be My Age?

Everywhere I look I come across evidence of my antiquity. A week ago I visited my house outside Rome which is falling to bits and is going to cost a fortune to renovate. My manager told me that he was taking good care of it – but the house is very old. Well, I built the house: if it's decaying, what about me?

I got really angry and snarled something about the plane trees, which I had planted with my own hands and which now resembled leafless arthritic joints with mottled skin. My manager swore up and down that he was doing his utmost, but the trees were just old.

Then an ancient man in the last throes of decrepitude appeared at the door – and I capped the day's misadventures by exclaiming: 'Who on earth is *that*? He looks as if he's risen from the dead!'

At this the poor chap turned incredulous eyes on me and said: 'Don't you recognise me? You used to bring me little acorns. I'm the son of your former manager. I'm the boy you used to play with every day.'

So my weekend retreat has helped me by turning into a hall of mirrors. I vowed to stop playing the fool to myself and accept my extreme maturity. Old age is full of pleasures when you know how to cherish it.

❖ None of us is the same the next morning as we were the night before; the same old as we were young. Every instant is the death of the moment that preceded it.
❖ Those who forget the past, who neglect the present and fear the future have brief and discontented lives.
❖ All things to come are uncertain. Live now!

When a by no means guaranteed future kills the bright today...

❖ Foresight, the greatest blessing humanity has been given, is transformed into a curse by fear.
❖ The major obstacle to living is expectation, which depends on tomorrow while it squanders today.
❖ We hang on the future if there's no fulfilment in the present.
❖ None of us can make ourselves promises about what is to come. Even what we hold slips through our fingers; and accident cuts short the very hour we have in our grasp. Fear keeps pace with hope, like a prisoner and his escort.

- ❖ Shall I plot and save, oblivious to my mortality?
- ❖ They live ill who are always beginning to live.
- ❖ You can't spend life in readying yourself to live.
- ❖ The life of the fool is replete with misgivings and humiliations, for its goal is never now, but the future.

Use Your Life: Don't Hoard It: a Story

As far as their wealth is concerned, people are often stingy. Yet when it comes to wasting time, the sole area in life where you should be miserly, they are wanton.

Think about how much time is taken with the bank, how much with a lover, how much with a boss or an assistant. How much in rowing with your partner, how much in throwing yourself round and round the social round.

Add to these illnesses caused by the way we live, as well as the time that has hung about unused. You'll see that you've fewer years than you thought you had.

Cast your mind over the past: how many days did you spend as you had hoped, when you were really doing what you wanted to do, and not what others did? When the expression on your face wasn't merely a social grimace, when – above all! – your spirit was calm. Think about the work you've achieved in your life. How much of your time was spent in gratuitous gloom? In joy for the wrong things, in guilty desires? How little was left for you! However many your years, you're dying before your time.

- ❖ The point is not to live too long but to live enough.
- ❖ The life we receive is not short – but we make it short. It needn't be meagre in quality – but we waste it.
- ❖ It can be true that the person who has lived long has lived too little.
- ❖ No one is so old that it's unnatural of them to hope to live another day.
- ❖ Every day should be ordered as if it were our last, as if it were the one that rounds out and completes our lives.
- ❖ Be responsible to yourself. Gather up and store the time that was stolen from you. Yes, this is the truth: some moments are torn from us, others merely ebb away. But there's no worse loss than that due to carelessness. Get a grip on today and you'll find you're less anxious about tomorrow. While we put off and postpone forever, life dances past, waving goodbye as if it belonged to someone else. The last day ends it – and everyday in between wastes it.
- ❖ Even if we were totally awake, life would rush in front of us; as it is, we drag our heels, and it waves goodbye as if it belonged to someone else. The last day ends it; and every day in between wastes it.

Ripeness is all.

Train yourself to recognise the moment. What good is it to have succeeded in making friends of your impulses and desires if when the stage is set for action, you're blind to when, where, and how to act?

For it's one thing to know the value of things; and

quite another to recognise emergencies; and yet another to know how to go calmly into the fray instead of rushing ahead wildly.

How Do You Measure Long? Put Away Your Ruler: a Story

Life, if you know how to live it, is long. But one person is possessed by insatiable greed, another by work; one by booze, another by laziness. This soul is impaled by ambition and the opinions of others; that one is harassed by the idea of danger to herself and so is always inflicting it on other people. Very many are exhausted by continuously making new plans, and others have no principles by which to live. All of these Death takes unaware while they yawn.

❖ When we say we've lived enough we should measure not the years but the spirit.
❖ A contented life is not possible for those who think too much about prolonging it.
❖ The length of our lives is not under our control. Its reality is ours to shape.
❖ Life is never incomplete if it's based on ethics: stop at any point and it's whole.
❖ Make every day a life in miniature.

And Memory, Too: a Story

Wild animals run from the dangers they apprehend through their senses and, once they've escaped, forget them. We humans, however, are tormented not only by what is past but by what is to come. Memory replays for us the torture of being afraid; while anticipation brings it on prematurely. None of us confines our unhappiness to the present.

Put a ban on all handwringing over past woes. Yes, perhaps you suffered badly then – but now it's over. What possible good can come from being unhappy now, merely because you were unhappy then?

❖ Two distresses of the mind must be eliminated. One is the fear of suffering in the future; the other is the memory of past suffering. The first should no longer concern you; the second has not yet happened, and may never happen.

❖ Life is divided into three periods: that which has gone, that which is now, and that which will be. Of these three, the present is short and the future, dubious. Only the past is certain.

So we must remember…
You cannot bring back the years. No one will give you again to yourself. Life will go along the road it began, and can neither reverse nor stop its course. It is silent: it won't alert you to the swiftness of its passing. But Death is waiting, for which you must find time.

6

Life's a Lottery:
A Throw of the Dice Won't
Abolish Chance

There is only a moment between sitting on one throne and kneeling to another.

Chance conquers us, unless we conquer it.

Keep Chance your opponent. What Seneca learned:
'I never trusted Fortune, even when she seemed to be offering me peace. She gave me many blessings: high office, influence and wealth. Between these blessings and myself I drew a boundary, so that they could be taken away without injuring me. When Fortune turns hostile, no one can be crushed who hasn't first been seduced by her tricks.

❖ Why should I nag at Chance to give, rather than decide to finish seeking?
❖ If I yield to pleasure, I must also yield to pain; yield to grief, uncertainty, stress and anger. I shall be torn apart by this mob of emotions. Freedom is my goal.

What is freedom? The ability to be the slave of nothing and no one, to meet whatever happens head on.

Snapshot of us all
Have you ever seen a dog stretching its jaws wide open to grab scraps tossed by its master? What it catches, it swallows whole in a gulp. Then it opens its mouth again in slavering anticipation. We are that dog. We wait expectantly, open-mouthed, drooling. Whatever chance can fling at us we swallow instantly – tense and eager, ready to snap at the next scrap.

If Chance makes a toy of our lives, our principles must guide and protect us.

❖ Think how pleasant it is to ask for nothing, how wonderful to be complete in ourselves and independent of whatever vagaries life throws our way.

❖ The whirl of events will spin us into despair, unless we give up our expectations.

❖ It could be that all worldly treasures are heaped upon us. But goodness will never come our way by Chance.

❖ Avoid things that are the gifts of Fortune. When you receive a stroke of luck, stop suspiciously in alarm. The landscape fills with glorious views that will be your undoing. These are not gifts, but snares. We believe we've reached the top of the mountain. But Fortune doesn't just throw us down the mountain, it opens an abyss.

*What is now is not forever: the higher you rise, the lower
you fall.*
To maintain prosperity more prosperity is necessary; and
for the prayers that were answered yet more prayers are
needed.

*Do you think you're so different from that beggar in the street?
Whatever happens to one of us can happen to us all.*

❖ Chance has as much power over the lives of the rich
  as those of the poor.
❖ Those you call your inferiors can trace their begin-
  nings back to the same origin as you. They share the
  same sky above, they breathe in the same way, and
  they die just as you do. You may see them happy and
  prosperous; they may see you sad and ill – the odds
  are even. There is only a difference of birth.

*What we thought was catastrophe became a blessing. But the
events we welcomed with shouts of gladness destroyed us.*

7

Have a Rich Illness

Seneca's Own Story

When I was young I suffered a terrifying period of ill-health. At first I underplayed how really ill I was; but eventually I reached a state of complete collapse. There were many moments when I wanted to kill myself, but then I would think about my father, who had been nothing but kind to me and was an old man. His spirit would have been broken by the loss of me, so I told myself to live. Sometimes just to live is an act of courage.

What relieved me during those dreadful times were thoughts. Comforting images and ideas can be as healing as medical treatment, for the things that bring you mental rest benefit you physically as well.

My friends also made a major contribution to my cure. They cheered me on, spent hours by my bedside and distracted me by talk. They were a godsend. The devotion of friends is a corrective to the thought that you can bear things no longer.

I came to believe that I couldn't be dying while I was leaving my friends to survive me; and I also felt that if I couldn't continue to live among them, I could live through them. I wasn't giving up my soul but passing it on. These feelings gave me the will to live and endure. And besides, once you have conquered the desire to die, it's pathetic not to want to live.

But my studies of Stoicism were what really saved me; and I credit the fact that I was finally able to leave my bed to philosophy. I owe philosophy my life.

*

What I've been saying is that you have remedies for your illnesses waiting for you in your own mind or near to hand in your life. Your doctor may tell you how far you should walk, what exercise you can do, and not to over-do resting (which is a tendency with invalids), and he'll recommend a diet. He may urge you, as mine did, to read aloud to help your breathing.

But I'll give you my own prescription – not only for your current illness but for your whole life. It is: Despise death. Once you've genuinely escaped the fear of it, there's no more anxiety, depression or despair.

The mind–body connection from 2,000 years ago

❖ If you are content in mind, your body will suffer less in illness.

❖ Everything depends on how we think about it. Not only public notions like power and wealth are shaped by popular ideas: we take our cue from others even in the way we feel pain. So when you're ill, don't augment your troubles by fretting: instead, give yourself encouragement.

Illness has enabled people to renew and re-invent themselves.
The experience of nearly dying has been their salvation.

Other rousing thoughts on being ill

❖ Here's something you can achieve in illness: put up a good fight. If its threats leave you cold, you're setting others an impressive example.

❖ Let us unleash ourselves as much as we can from our bodies, the frail and complaining part of ourselves, and engage ourselves with our minds. That way, when illness comes, we have an anchor.

❖ It's our bodies and not our brains that are ailing when we're ill. If we normally have an active mind, we'll still be able to listen and learn and think.

And every bit of life's a stage...

❖ If only we ill people could live our illness before an audience! What proof of glory would be ours! Therefore, be your own audience, your own applauding admirer.

A Little Story

People will pity you for not being able to eat and drink all the rich and luxurious things when you're ill. 'How very unfortunate he is to be sick!' they'll exclaim. In reality, you'll be eating just as much as you can digest. Oysters won't be flinging themselves out of their shells on to your plate. You won't be icing cocktails in elegant glasses. There won't be a cooked dead animal lying in state in a place where people can admire it; nor will you have your trolley heaped with elaborate puddings swimming in sauces. But what's so terrible about being deprived of that? You'll be eating the dinner of an ill person: more precisely, you'll finally be eating the meal that a healthy person should eat.

And it may help to remember...

❖ When you die, it will be not because you are sick but because you were alive.

8

Love and Friendship: a Gathering of Sometimes Conflicting Ideas on a Tricky Subject

Individually we are neither successes nor failures. We live for a common end.

What Hecato said to me:
'I've made great progress. I'm beginning to be my own friend.' This is indeed a great advance. This man will never be alone. Everyone will want him as a friend.

❖ You must live for others if you want to live for yourself.
❖ If you believe someone to be loyal, you will make him so.
❖ Regard a friend as you would yourself.
❖ A friend may be made of an enemy.

Is this love?

❖ The feeling lovers hold for one another resembles friendship in some ways: you could call it friendship on a ride to the madhouse.

❖ This works better than brews from the medicine man: If you would be loved, love.

❖ No one can be blind to the usefulness of the hands. But the heart, from which the hands draw life and purpose, is unseen.

Friends: a situation comedy?

❖ It is wise to choose your friends for their goodness and avoid disturbed, wild and gloomy people.

❖ And avoid carelessness in choosing your friends. They should be worth the gift of our devotion.

❖ However, you must be practical. It would be impossibly limiting to associate only with people of talent and intellect and wisdom and humanity who can also tell a good joke. Where will you find all these people, or all these qualities in one person?

❖ In place of the idealised person, we should seek out the least bad.

Your friends are also your guides.
Make friends of those who are likely to improve you in some way. Welcome those whom you can improve. The process is mutual: we learn as we teach.

A warning

❖ Those who befriend you because it serves their purpose will cease to be a friend for the same reason.

❖ Take your friends' advice, but use your own counsel.

❖ Trust should follow friendship, and judgement go before that.

- ❖ If people can't talk about you to your face they'll do so behind your back.
- ❖ Some people are abusers and you'll find there is a charge for their friendship.

A quick word on enemies or bad people

- ❖ The bad are never in such a grim state as when their individual inadequacies are pooled.
- ❖ Those below us on the social scale are not our enemies but we make them so.
- ❖ To be feared is to feel fear.
- ❖ Whoever holds his own life in contempt is master of yours.
- ❖ Malice is the result of unproductiveness and disappointment. Because you cannot prosper, you wish ruin on everyone.

And when it ends in tears...
It is best to be armed when agreeing terms with our enemies. We will be safer and more highly regarded.

You can live for no one else, and yet not for yourself either. Dropping out and cocooning.

- ❖ If you can, before you put food on your table, look for people to place around it, for solitary stuffing is the life of the forest, the lion and the wolf.
- ❖ To isolate yourself from other people is to lose interest in the world and the possibility of worthwhile activity within it.

❖ The person who runs away from the world and other people, banishing himself by the failure of his dreams, unable to bear the sight of people luckier than he is, bolting for his hole, doesn't succeed in living for himself, but for his food, his bed and his passions.

People who need people... but first...

This is what Democritus wrote: One person means as much to me as a multitude, and a multitude as much as one person.

❖ Just as we're born with the taste for sweets, so it is with the taste for friendship.
❖ The feeling of communality that makes you human is the solid foundation of friendship.
❖ Friendship creates a bond of shared interests which further unites us.
❖ Treat those for whom Chance hasn't been as good as it's been to you in the way that you would like to be treated by those for whom Chance has been better.

Do we not all bleed? I am human: all that is human I hold kin.

❖ Why not pull together your brief life and make it peaceful both to yourself and to others? Why not make yourself beloved while you live, and mourned when you die?
❖ We are all members of the universe, both physical and spiritual. We all come from the same source. Nature has encoded in us the instinct to love one another and

to create unity. This is the thought we should hold in our hearts:

As long as we draw breath
As long as we live among people
Let us cherish one another.

Let us not bring fear or danger to anyone; let us forgive wrongs and oppressions and endure our pains. In the moment that we turn around and look back, death has arrived.

Our shared humanity is like an arch
that would collapse
without the interlocking of the stones
which just by interlocking
hold the arch in place.

9

Anger, Rage and Rages

A Story of Roman Rage and Cruelty

Incensed by the sight of a well-bred young dandy with elaborate hair, the emperor Caligula sent him to prison. When the father begged that his son might be released, the emperor gave orders that the handsome young man be executed immediately.

But in order to appear to be humane to the father, Caligula invited him to dine with him that evening. The father arrived and betrayed no anger or reproach. Taking a cup, the emperor toasted the poor man, who went through with the charade, though it seemed to him that he was swallowing the blood of his son.

And do you ask why he behaved in this way? The man had a second son. Therefore he carried to his lips the murderous royal hand and dined and drank to his own health and curbed his rage and sorrow, not for his own sake, but for that of his remaining child. Far from it being to our advantage to avenge wrongs, it is often dangerous, and usually damaging, even to acknowledge them.

Anger is a useless emotion. It blocks its own progress towards the goals to which it hurtles.

❖ Rage is temporary insanity.
❖ Rage is fearful. It comes not only when we've been hurt, but when we believe someone is intending to hurt us.
❖ Everyone possesses the power to harm others.
❖ You can choose to get angry – or not to get angry.
❖ The primary characteristic of rage is wilfulness. It is as futile an aid to reason as the soldier who ignores the order to retreat.
❖ Anger makes calm seem like disorder; peace appear like war.
❖ Rage is rash. Although it seeks to harm others, it doesn't guard against its own injuries.
❖ The most likely outcome of rage is self-destruction.

Collective anger is war.
Of all the vices, it is rage alone that can possess a whole country. No whole populace has ever burned unanimously with love for a particular woman; and no entire territory has supported one greedy ambition. Only rage is a mass affliction.

Remember:
Our natural state is peaceful and calm, and shuns those things that provoke anger and disorder.

A snapshot of rage by a philosopher who was also a playwright
Behold rage: a threatening manner, a quick, irregular step, nervous hand movements, rapid and violent

breaths. The eyes burn and send out flares, the face reddens with blood that flows from the lowest depths of the heart, the lips tremble, the teeth clench, the hair bristles and appears to stand on end, the body writhes awkwardly, joints cracking.

The sufferer shouts; strange cries, groans and pre-language emerge along with strangled words; he stamps the ground and the whole over-excited body instinctively makes strange threatening shapes.

It is impossible to know whether rage is more disgusting for being morally deplorable or for being aesthetically hideous.

How spoilt we are! Road rage, pavement rage, parking-meter rage, surf rage, computer rage, air rage, sex rage, parent rage, child rage, queue rage, you rage.

We're not hurt by everything that fails to satisfy our will completely or isn't entirely perfect for us.

Yet our lives of being pampered children propel us into tantrums, where anything that isn't all we dreamed unhinges us.

Bullying: an epidemic

- ❖ No one has ever been made braver by rage, except those bullies who would only have been cowards without it.
- ❖ For those seeking power, a presumed grievance is the pretext for aggression.
- ❖ Brutality always has its origins in weakness. Kindness originates in strength.

So you want revenge?

- ❖ No emotion is keener on revenge than rage. And for that reason it is unfit to take it.
- ❖ If you take no pleasure in anger you won't desire revenge, which takes pleasure in punishment.
- ❖ We think that feeling anger on behalf of those we love, or the oppressed, be they human or animal, is noble. It's not. What is noble and also effective is to defend what we love and believe by calmness and good judgement.

Another snapshot

Just as someone thrown off a cliff has no control over his body and, speeding irrevocably down, is lost to all making-good of his life, and is now unavoidably thrown towards a fate he would have avoided, so too the mind: it plunges into anger and cannot stop its compulsion; and so it hurtles to the bottom.

Seneca knew all about guilt long before Dostoevsky.

Even if a crime is undiscovered, the perpetrator believes that detection could come at any moment. His nights are sweaty. When he hears that someone else is guilty of something, he immediately thinks of himself, for guilt is never far from his mind. The wrongdoer may go free all his life, but that is uncertain and he will never be free in his mind.

- ❖ Even the conscience of the lowest person insists on recognition.

- ❖ To earn punishment is to expect it. Your conscience will not let you off.
- ❖ You may find safety after a crime, but you will never feel safe.

Seneca didn't believe in capital punishment.
A good physician will begin a cure with the kindest measures. First, he will ask the patient to make changes in his routine. If no relief is obtained, he may tweak things here and there. He may suggest fasting. If this fails, he must take measures that are increasingly radical.

In the same way, a law-enforcer should begin to heal a troubled person by discussion, so that the wrongdoer may be persuaded to do what is right, and to believe that this is truly the best way of behaving; and to loathe what is wrong. If this doesn't succeed, the official can progress to the harsher language of castigation and reproof.

Finally he will have to punish – always bearing in mind that it should be the lightest form and never irrevocable.

A paradox on this subject
No one should be punished by death unless it benefits them to lose their life.

Rage: self-help

- ❖ The best corrective of anger is delay.
- ❖ Ask anger to wait – not so it can pardon, but so it may judge.
- ❖ Its first assaults are brutal; immobilise them.
- ❖ If you don't dismiss the first brewings of anger, it will

advance into the whole of your person, and all boundaries will be lost.

❖ Once anger has begun, the way back is difficult. It bullies and takes over, destroying reason, calm and, ultimately, sanity.

❖ You can't be angry and retain control of yourself at the same time.

❖ If you believe you've succeeded in not acting on your anger, it's usually because fear, or hope of a favour, or some other unworthy emotion has won.

❖ If you apply reason to anger and are patient, anger will disappear.

❖ Don't be quick to believe what others tell you: some people are trying to deceive you; while others are themselves deceived.

The story of how a philosopher handled rage: a word on self-punishment

Once, when Plato became enraged with his servant, he was unable to impose delay on himself. He ordered the servant to remove his shirt and bare his shoulders in readiness for a beating.

But just as he, Plato, the philosopher, raised his arm to deliver the first blow, he realised where rage had removed him. And he remained standing for hours, just as he was, with his arm in the air in the posture of striking.

A friend arrived and asked why he found the sage in this ridiculous position. Plato replied: 'I am punishing an angry man.' He had totally forgotten about the servant, and had found someone who needed punishment more.

10

Fear and Trembling and Courage

Did you realise only now that suffering and death are our companions? We were born to them: they are our mother and our father

Learn the reality of your fears and find the good in them

Fear Is a Fool's Game: a Necessarily Short Story

We fear certain things more than others. Yet life always ends the same way: with death. So, what difference does it make if it's a building or a mountain that topples over on us? Of course there's no difference. Yet you'll find people who are only terrified of the mountain. Fear is so stupid that it disregards the result and concentrates on the cause.

A lesson
Here's a way of shedding your terrors. Imagine that all the things that you're afraid of happening will occur no matter what you do. Evaluate all the harm that they each could bring. Assess your fears accordingly. What you'll discover is that the things you dread are either not so

large or not so long-lasting. You'll see how much more eager your courage is to anticipate suffering than the world's indifference to inflict it.

Fear is a disease...

❖ And it's infectious. One person's fear is caught by another, and so it builds.

❖ Many of our fears are only received ideas which look real because they haven't been refuted.

❖ Children become frightened of their friends when they see them in disguise. We bigger children suffer the same feelings. Not only people but events must have their masks torn off and their true features restored.

It was Seneca who said it first:

❖ Strip things of their appearances and look at what is essential. You'll find that the thing most to be feared is fear itself.

A comforting paradox

❖ Far from being our greatest terror, death is an event which heals our other terrors.

❖ Thanks to death, nothing is to be feared.

Lastly: let go.

Remind yourself that your body is fragile and vulnerable – and not only to external aggressions. Pleaures can lead to pain: rich meals and drink to illness; you can be allergic to the finest foods and scents. Say to your yourself: I shall become a poor person: I shall become one of the majority.

Or
I shall be imprisoned. So what? Am I really so free now? Nature has bound me to this encumbrance of a body. I shall die. What I mean is: I shall stop being liable to illness. I shall cease being vulnerable to oppression. I shall no longer be frightened of death.

A final exercise for the expunging of fear
Regard hypothetical terrors as inevitable.

Courage: a Short Lesson from History

❖ Not only heroes have met death with equanimity. Even those who were cowards have behaved splendidly when their end came.

Such a person was Scipio, the commander of many victories. When he was propelled by an evil wind back into enemy territory, he ran himself through with his sword. As he lay dying, the enemy boarded the ship and asked, 'Where's the captain?'

'Safe!' he exclaimed; and with this word he died. It had been a tremendous achievement to conquer Cathage; but it was an even greater one to vanquish death.

❖ Of course no one can be completely impervious to

external events. We automatically grimace at something sour, jump at anything sudden, and go dizzy if we stand on the edge of a cliff and look down. These aren't the symptoms of fear, but physical reactions beyond reason. In this way, nature reminds us of our mortality.

❖ We often create problems we should be guarding against. When something is bearing down heavily, about to fall and crush us, it becomes more dangerous if we back away, for it will only move towards us and become even heavier. But if instead you stand fiirm and resist, it can be forced back.

❖ To be an exceptional person, you must encounter difficulty in life, for only then can you be courageous.

Here is another metaphor:

❖ Say you are suffering severe mental or physical pain. Do you really think you'll appease it by complaining? Just as in war the enemy does greater harm to retreating troops, so every trouble weighs more heavily on the person who has turned his back on it and is giving up.

And another:

❖ Look at the example of boxers and wrestlers. They will put up with any amount of pain, not only in performance, but in training, for the glory of winning. Let us also overcome all blows. Instead of fame, we'll win the strength of mind that results from giving a particularly difficult struggle your best shot.

When you're buried by difficulties, you'll find relief by step-ping away from them and turning your mind elsewhere. Think about the things you've done in the past that you consider most courageous: play over in your memory your finest moments. This will encourage you and give you strength.

11

Adversity

Mastering Patience: a Story

I arrived at my house in Alba completely exhausted by the journey – which was thoroughly uncomfortable for an old man like me, thrashed about in that heaving carriage. And what do you know? Nothing was ready for my arrival – apart from myself. So I'm writing to you from my old man's bed (which is of course unmade), resting, unbathed (for there's no water) and so tired that I'm not all that sorry that the baker and the cook (now that we've located them!) are slower than snails.

All these difficulties have made me aware again of how calm life is if you don't take its inconveniences to heart, and how we wear ourselves out by magnifying our irritations.

It's indeed true that my baker has no bread – but perhaps the farm manager will have some, or a tenant, or the steward. 'Not very nice bread, though,' you'll say. But wait a minute: it will soon transform itself by hunger into food fit for a king. So I'll wait to eat until I have my own bread or hunger makes me less picky.

We must teach ourselves to bear with things. You could be enormously rich, with a flotilla of servants, and still be mown down by difficulties thrown your way. None of us can have everything we want: but we can refrain from wanting what we haven't got, and tranquilly make the best of what's to hand. Tonight's culinary improvisation just might be more tasty, and will certainly be less monotonous, than the dinner I had anticipated. Perhaps freedom consists of a stomach that knows when to be quiet.

The destiny of people or of countries rolls on, whatever we may do. Suddenly in peace war breaks out, and misfortune appears around the least expected corner. Kingdoms which held up during civil wars are destroyed by a sigh. It follows that we must keep our eyes open and fortify ourselves against any possibility. Reflect upon sickness, war, catastrophe.

When you're in the thick of your troubles you should tell yourself, as Virgil said: Even these bitter events may one day make a sweet memory.

Be prepared: You should know that there are many things you will have to endure. The mind will meet bravely everything it has anticipated.

❖ It's on those who expect nothing but good luck that disaster falls most heavily.

❖ Unfamiliarity deepens misfortune. There never was a person whose troubles weren't compounded by surprise.

❖ All life is warfare. The people in the thick of it are valiant. But the cushioned safety of those who loll about marks them out for trouble.

Think of your troubles as training.

❖ Take in good part whatever happens, and turn it to your advantage.

❖ It is not what you endure, but how you endure that is important.

❖ Good people are willing that bad things should happen. If you are unwilling you call upon misfortune.

❖ You may wonder why people suffer atrocious misfortunes. But if you're surprised that these events could be for anyone's benefit, then you must also be surprised that by unpleasant treatment, the sick are frequently made well.

❖ Adversity is often to the good of those to whom it comes, just as the things which are most sought after are frequently to the detriment of those who receive them.

❖ Familiarity with danger will give us contempt for it.

❖ There is pleasure in being able to survive something which was very harsh: one should congratulate oneself and take the time to rejoice that it's over.

To be always happy and to pass through life without suffering is to be ignorant of the condition of being human: you have sailed through life without an enemy and no one will know what you're capable of, least of all yourself.

Testing: You are unfortunate who have always been fortunate.

❖ Disaster is virtue's opportunity.
❖ Misfortune weighs hardest on the inexperienced. The new recruit pales at the idea of a wound, but the veteran is undaunted by his own blood. He knows that suffering is usually the price of victory.
❖ Those who float in the calm of good fortune are doomed; for whatever happens will come to them as a change.

Good luck never made a fool wise.

❖ Your best luck is not to need luck.
❖ Of all excesses the most harmful is unlimited ease of life.
❖ If you think less about luck, you'll find it by your side.
❖ You are wrong if you imagine that anyone is exempt from trouble. Even the prosperous will some day have their share. Those who enjoy good fortune have only been reprieved.
❖ The things given to us by luck cannot be owned forever.
❖ Magnificent blessings are rarely long-lasting. Those that come slowly with hard work are more likely to go with us to the end.

The most golden rule:
Today proves me wrong if it treats me kindly. But this isn't entirely true, for as much as I know that disaster can befall me, I am aware that it is not inevitable.

12

Your Richness Is Inside You:
Mine Your Own Gold

Noise and Noises of the Mind: a Story

Here I am in the midst of a yowling babel. I'm living over
a public bath-house. I can hear every grunt as my neighbours lift weights and even the hissings and gasps as
they let out their breaths. When they're finished and having a massage, not only is the smack of a hand on flesh
faithfully transmitted to my ears, but even the variety of
notes, depending whether the hand is flat or cupped and
where it is on the body.

You can take it from there. The shouts of the score-
keepers, the splash of someone leaping into the pool, the
shrill yelps of those having their underarms plucked. On
top of all this, the rough cries, each one quite distinctive,
of the men selling food and drink. It's a madhouse.

But I swear I take no notice of this cornucopia of
sounds. There can be an absolute storm outside as long
as there's calmness inside, as long as desires and fears
are kept from quarrelling. For what's the good of having
silence all down the street if your emotions are loud and
discordant?

❖ Men and birds together in full chorus will never disturb our thinking when that thinking is solid and good and steady.

A Shorter Noise Story

Look at the rich person who lives in a grand house with no neighbours. Let's say he can impose absolute silence. Naturally, night finds him tossing from side to side, desperate to catch a little sleep, obsessed with noises that aren't there. And where are the noises? They're in his mind, which is in ferment. It's his mind which needs to be at peace. Here's the war that cries out for a peace-making mission.

What is it to be happy? It is freedom from enslavement to yourself or to the things outside you.

❖ The happiest person is the one who is independent of his own happiness. The most powerful is that person who has himself in his own power.
❖ Happiness generated by itself, without need of material things, is solid and trustworthy. It keeps on growing and accompanies us right to the end.

A longer definition
Happiness is a by-product of sound living. It can't be attained as an end in itself. Chase after it and it vanishes: for that is the best way to invite it to elude you.

Another long definiton
What we're seeking is how we may always pursue a helpful path and find harmony within ourselves, and continue in this way without interruption, without violent swings and dissents and falls, always in a state of peace.

And now a question...
We know that we have a soul. But what that is – its source, its home, its duration – that we don't know. We understand that there's something in all of us that moves us, but we're ignorant of what that is. And we know we have power, but we are unaware of its source.

❖ From any darkness we may leap up to the best.
❖ Seeds of divinity are scattered in our bodies; we can make them bloom.
❖ The good person is never without something we may call the divine.

A diamond rule
Let food satisfy hunger, drink quench thirst. Let sexual desire follow its natural course. Let's learn to increase our self-control, to moderate ambition, to soften anger, to cultivate simpler things and move in the direction of our instincts. Let's keep mad hope and the habit of thinking only to the future in chains. Let us seek our riches from ourselves.

I'm going to contradict your parents...
who prayed that you might have wealth and riches. Their prayers rob others, for what you receive must be

taken from someone else. But I, on the other hand, wish you possession of yourself: that your mind, beset by worries and fleeting thoughts, may finally become peaceful and find satisfaction in itself.

The happy life is one that has been established slowly and steadily on correct judgement.

Vacillation Makes You Miserable and a Ham Actor: a Story

The most obvious symptom of a soul in distress is restlessness. You waver between a pretence of goodness and a craving for illicit pleasures. What you want changes every day: one day, it's a spouse; the next, a lover. Now you decide it would be amusing to be king; tomorrow, that the only way to live honestly is to be the most menial worker.

The hour arrives when you're so inflated with self-importance that you resemble a toad. The next morning you're so abject you can't stand upright. One moment you're throwing money around; afterwards, you're on your knees scrambling for it. You fool the world into believing that you're a serious and even ascetic person; then you're partying, spendthrift and frivolous.

Moment by moment we change our masks, ripping off the clown to reveal the tragedian. Therefore, decide to keep your true character to the end.

If you can't succeed at that, at least make yourself recognisable.

Steady on...
So you need to have something to worry about? Can't you see that your worrying and bother is all that is wrong with you?

A Small Story

So I am not well: not unusual. All the people I rely on are off work, my money is running out, the house is falling down. Losses, wounds, grievances, griefs, terrors assail me. What else is new? It's not only the usual: it's the inevitable.

Another question
What is it that drags us in one direction when we're straining to go the other way, and forces us back to the place we wanted to leave? What is it that battles with our minds and prevents us from exercising our will?

More on vacillation
Some people live frugally at home, but go for broke outside it. Some eat meanly but furnish their houses with eye-blasting ostentation. Inconsistency is a weakness, a symptom of an ill-balanced mind which is looking for its true path.

Do you want to be a slave?
I can show you a high-placed former government official in hock to a little old lady, his mother; a billionaire to his chauffeur; a royal who is the chattel of a ballet dancer. No

slavery is more degrading than voluntary bondage. Freedom is something we give to ourselves.

An experiment
We all like to say that we didn't choose our parents. But we can choose the people whose children we'd like to be. There are families of the noblest minds. Choose the one into which you'd like to be adopted, and you will inherit their spiritual wealth.

A bit of a rant
The human brain can look beyond our little world to wonder at the heavens. But we have torn our minds away from this divine spectacle and dragged ourselves down to rut in the sty, to enslave ourselves to greed, to forsake large thoughts, and to snuffle underground for any vermin we can find.

A final experiment: flex your will as you would your muscles.
So many people exercise their bodies and forget about their minds. Enormous crowds cram the sports stadia but ignore the libraries. This is the question: if the body can be trained to such an ideal of strength that it can take punches and kicks, how much more easily can the spirit be empowered to withstand the blows of chance without collapsing, and to stand tall again after it has been thrown to the ground and trampled? For although the body needs many different kinds of nourishment, the spirit is capable of feeding and training itself, of growing from within. Athletes require food and drink, massages and long hours of training. Contentment can be yours

without equipment or cost. You have everything for it within you. What extra do you need? The will.

13

As Long as You Live You Must Keep Learning

A Game of Chess or Thank You for Ordering My Execution

A dictator concluded an argument with a philosopher by informing him that the learned sage was to be executed. The philosopher merely replied: 'Your Excellency, I give you my thanks.'

Why did he answer in this way? Did he mean to be insulting? Or was he accepting death as a welcome escape from this madman, who had killed many people? Whatever the reason, it was a big-hearted reply.

The philosopher, who was called Julius Canus, spent the ten days before his execution in total calm. He was playing chess when the centurion who was dragging away the day's consignment of the condemned ordered the philosopher to join them.

Canus reacted by turning to the chessboard and counting the pawns. To his co-player he said: 'Make certain that after I die you don't claim you've won the game.' He then told the centurion to bear witness that he, Canus, was one pawn ahead.

Canus was not acting a part. Rather, it was the centurion who was afraid.

His friends were full of grief at his impending death. So he asked them: 'Why are you so sad? Everyone wonders whether our souls are immortal. But I shall know the answer very soon.'

Up to the very end he made his death a subject for debate – searching for truth. His teacher asked him how he was feeling. Canus replied: 'I am determined to keep watch to see whether the spirit will know that it's leaving the body when the moment of death arrives.' He promised that if he made any discoveries, he would find a way of revealing to his friends the truth about the immortality of the soul.

Here is a spirit that seeks to learn even from death itself. You can't be a philosopher for longer than that.

Some of Seneca's thoughts on Stoic philosophy

❖ What is philosophy but an encyclopaedia of the laws of living?
❖ It's by the grace of Heaven that we live; and by philosophy's bounty that we live well.
❖ I'll tell you what philosophy offers us: the blessings of counsel and consolation.
❖ Philosophy must provide a set of formulated principles. You ask why? Because it is through principles that we embrace the whole of worldly life and beyond, that we discover strength and peace of mind.
❖ Philosophy combines theory and practice, contemplation and action.

❖ The promise of philosophy is unity with all human beings.

A thought: Many people would have attained wisdom if they hadn't imagined they had already achieved it.

More on Wisdom

❖ Continue to learn as long as you remain ignorant — that is, until the end of your life. Or to put it another way: as long as you live you must keep learning how to live.

❖ Learning is large and generous: it needs space. There are lessons about past and present, the temporary and the eternal, Heaven and Earth.

❖ This is how I would like to fill my mind: Let it be furnished with knowledge, with sound rules, with historical examples — all blended together as a whole fabric. How can I do this? By using my reason.

❖ If you apply yourself to learning you will avoid boredom with life. You will never find yourself longing for night because you can't manage the day. You will attract the finest people to you. In this way, you will doubly enrich your life.

❖ The enthusiasm for learning must be contained in method. You shouldn't skim aimlessly, nor madly try to corral knowledge in bulk. The whole can be reached only through its parts.

❖ The more your mind absorbs, the more it expands.

❖ Why do we give our children an education? Not because in itself it can make them moral beings, but because it prepares their minds for understanding morality.

Even a Philosopher Needs to Dream: Seneca Finds a Golden Age in the Past: a Story

The first people on Earth took one of them as their leader and freely submitted to this person of superior merit. So at this time, which we refer to as the Golden Age, power was vested in wise men and women. They protected the weak from the strong, advised on what was good and bad, and preserved peace. Their courage fought off danger and their compassion brought contentment and prosperity to their subjects. The purpose of the government was to serve, not to rule. The leaders could hold no more terrifying threat over their subjects than to menace them with their abdication.

Nevertheless...
From no age are we barred: we have access to them all, and if we wish there's a huge stretch of time through which we can wander. We may argue with Socrates, conquer human nature with the Stoics, rejoice with Epicurus, debate with Aristotle. Why shouldn't we turn away from our meagre span of time and enjoy the past, which is infinite, and which we can easily share with our betters?

Learning is no snob.

❖ Top of philosophy's values is its indifference to your ancestry.

❖ It's not through your class that philosophy admits you. Socrates was not an aristocrat. Cleanthes earned his living by watering a garden. Philosophy didn't find Plato noble: she made him noble. These men are all your ancestors, if you live properly.

What I said to the musician…
You can teach me how treble and bass clefs can harmonise, and how strings creating a variety of notes produce harmony. But before learning that, I'd prefer to know how to have harmony in my soul and in my desires. You can show me the minor keys; but it would be better if you could teach me to abjure the key of lamentation when troubles come.

A Little Story

Even as an old man I haven't stopped my reading, which I need to do so I won't be too satisfied with myself, and to make me capable of judging others' opinions. Reading refreshes and nourishes. But we must write as well. It's best to do each in turn, so that the results of one can be blended in the other.

Stick around those who can teach you something.
The person who goes out in the sun, though she may not go out for this purpose, gets sunburnt; another who has sat in a perfume shop will carry the scent of the place with her; and that person who has been in the company of a good thinker, as long as she is not hostile, even if she is inattentive, will have learned something.

❖ Choose as your teacher the person who commands your admiration more by what you see than by what you hear.

❖ Pleasure in learning comes partly from the fact that it enables us to teach. No knowledge can do good if its purpose is solely to serve itself.

❖ If wisdom were offered to me only on condition that I keep it hidden within myself, I would refuse it. There's no pleasure in owning anything that is unshared.

But remember...

There are those who can measure even the spaces in the heavens. But can they measure someone's soul? How large or small it is? Some can detect distances between planets. But what use is that if they can't calculate the distance between what we say and what we mean, what is real and what is not?

❖ The geometrician teaches me how to hold on to every fraction of my land, but what I need to learn is how to lose it all – and not lose my head.

❖ What use is maths to me if I'm unable to divide my land with a brother?

14

Have a Rich Death

And how can you teach humanity that death is no evil? How can you dispel beliefs as old as time? What curb on human weakness can you discover? How can you vanquish this consensus of dread?

Suicide: a Story

A man of high office, who had found happiness early in his life, began thinking about suicide when in old age he contracted a tedious disease.

He called together his friends, all of whom gave useless advice, except one, a Stoic, who said: 'My dear man, you mustn't think this is an enormous decision. To live is not extraordinary – your servants and animals do it. But to die honourably and splendidly – now, that is rare.

'Just think about the length of time you've been continually performing the same activities: eat, sleep, have sex – the endless cycle. Your wish to die may be caused not by honourable motives, but by boredom.'

The official needed no weapon or dramatic act to accomplish his death. First, he fasted. Then he ordered a tent with a bath inside it to be placed in his bedroom.

He lay in the bath for several days in hot water which was constantly renewed. And so almost imperceptibly he passed away, aware, as he said, only of a slow and peaceful fall into a state of unconsciousness. His chosen death was a soothing gliding out of life.

When we finally arrive at death we've been on a journey to that destination for a long time.

It isn't the last drop of sand that empties the hourglass.

❖ The death we fear is our last and not our only death.
❖ We die every day: for daily a portion of our lives is taken from us. Even when we are small and growing bigger, our lives are growing shorter. We have lost in succession infancy, childhood and youth. All the time that has passed up to yesterday is now lost; and this day we share with death.

So you won't be lonely.
You were born to death. It was the fate of your father, your mother and of all who came before you. It will be the fate of those who follow you.

What is the harm in returning to the place where you came from? Consolation by logic.

❖ It's the same thing. You were not; and you won't be.
❖ Death is all that was before we came on this earth. How can it matter if you cease to be or if you never begin, when the result of both is that you are not?

❖ Death either destroys or frees us. If we are freed, the best part of us remains, having lost its heavy burden of the body. If we are destroyed, then nothing at all remains, neither the good nor the bad.

And Grief...
To complain that someone has died is to complain because they were alive.

An explanation of fear
Though merely a fact, death wears the look of an abomination. For we all share a love of self, and an instinct for survival. Therefore we rebel against dissolution, because it removes us not only from what we consider good, but from what we know, and we have a horror of the unknown. And here is something else we don't like thinking about: our innate fear of the dark, into which, so we believe, death will take us. We ought to despise death, but we seldom do; because so many clever writers have imagined its horrors.

❖ It is true that often the cause of death is the fear of dying.

Always at hand is the end of things. At hand, I assure you, is the moment when the happy person is thrown out, and the unhappy one is allowed to go.

❖ Let us stop trembling at the thought of death. Let us desist from fearing death. Only when we conquer our fear will we be able to put an end to this malaise of being bored with living and afraid of dying.

You must know how to die well in order to live well. Those who don't know how to die well live badly.

The person who fears death will never do anything of greatness. But if you know that death is a precondition of being born, you will live on those terms and use them to honour your life.

A paradox

All that happens is chaotic and arbitrary and unpredictable. Yet we all distress ourselves over the single thing of which we can be assured.

A strange remedy for the fear of death

Practise death. To say this is to practise freedom. Those who learn how to die unlearn subservience to anything. They are beyond outside powers. What is a prison to them? They have an open door.

And another...

When we go we should say to Nature: take back a spirit that I've made better than when you gave it.

15

Remedies for the Well-being of the Soul

A Doleful Tale of the Sea: a Story

It was a mixed prognosis: the sea was still and glassy but the sky was streaked with the deep grey that signals rain. Anyway, I had only a short distance to travel; and I thought if we headed for the open water and avoided the twists of the shore, I stood a good chance of a safe and calm arrival.

But as soon as we had got too far out to turn back, the sweet stillness of the sea disappeared, and the fact that we were rocking rather violently up and down could not be ignored. I beseeched my captain to put me ashore – anywhere! But he informed me that this was foolhardy; and his own, more realistic fear was of being battered by a storm in a rocky cove.

But alas! By then I was too far gone in seasickness to care about anything so inessential as our lives. So I ordered the captain to make for land: I was desperate. And the moment it was remotely possible to swim for the shore, I dived into the rock-infested sea, still in my heavy garments, with the vague supposition that the experience would be similar to my medicinal cold baths. It was not. No one except a drowning man can imagine what it was like – competing with the spewing water and torrents of rain to find a passageway through the rocks and on to land.

When at last I crawled bleeding out of the sea, I bore the wounds of the sailor's belief that one does well to fear land as much as water. What I had had to endure through my deplorable failure to tolerate a bit of seasickness beggars belief.

When I had brought back some life into my frozen body, I began to reflect on humanity's great amnesia when it comes to remembering our weaknesses.

So it often happens that only when you're practically delirious with fever do you admit that there might be something wrong with you and cry for the doctor. And when your foot aches, you tell yourself it's only a sprained muscle. As long as the ailment stays in the initial stages, we don't dare to name it. When it becomes full-blown, we shout: GOUT! BROKEN BONE! HELP! from the rooftops.

Luckily, my captain was uninjured. But that's one boat we'll never use again.

First step: Shake hands with your lesser self and recognise what ails you.

❖ In the moment we perceive ourselves as being ill, we begin the cure.
❖ Knowledge of our mistakes is the beginning of salvation.

❖ We all know our own physical defects. But we pretend we don't know those of our souls. Some parts of them are sick and waiting to see the doctor.
❖ When it comes to spiritual afflictions, the worse you are, the less you know it. Why can't we admit our failings? The reason is that we're deeply trapped by them. For it's only when we've awakened that we know we were dreaming.

If you don't realise you are at fault, you refuse correction. Therefore, recognise that the failings you attributed to circumstance are actually your own. It's our habit to blame our shortcomings on the time or the place or on other people, but you'll find they follow you, wherever you go.

❖ It's when you think you're cured that you're most at risk.
❖ So this is the exercise: do your best to prove yourself guilty. Uncover the evidence against yourself. Be prosecutor, then judge, and finally mediator of your error.

Self-examination: a Story

Our minds should be directed to give an account of themselves at the end of every day.

One of my teachers followed this practice. When he had retired to bed, he would ask himself the following questions: Which failing have you overcome today? Which of your bad habits have you resisted? In what way are you better?

Can anything be better than this exercise of carefully sorting through the whole day?

All the useless emotions, especially rage, will quieten down and become manageable if they must appear before a judge. The sleep that follows after the soul has praised or admonished itself, when this secret examiner of the self has given its report, is deep, untroubled and delicious.

I avail myself of this privilege; and every night I plead my cause before the judge of myself. When the light is out, and my wife has become silent, I scan the whole of my day and retrace all my actions and words. I conceal nothing from myself; I omit nothing. In this way I needn't shrink from any of my mistakes. And this is the way I speak to myself: I will forgive you this time, but please see that you never do that again! In that argument, you spoke too aggressively; and now you've offended rather than helped. In the morning's discussion, you should have spoken more openly. Some form of praise to your colleague today would have been helpful. Why did I let that niggling worry spoil my contentment? Did I feel envious of my brother? Yes, and that was foolish and did me harm.

These are my musings. I can be as kind or as harsh as I like. But as with any judge, it is always better to err on the side of leniency. Then I sleep like a baby.

And every day also:

❖ Pray for a whole mind, for health of the spirit. Only after that, request bodily health.

- ❖ Be either cured or more curable.
- ❖ Acquire some idea which will help you cope with trouble. After you've thought through several ideas, select one to add permanently to your armoury.
- ❖ Take a step towards letting go of a bad habit.
- ❖ Strengthen your idea of wisdom by meditation. For you'll find it's harder to preserve a thought within yourself than it is to set one up as an ideal.

And very important: find a spirit guide.
Appoint a guardian over yourself. Honour that person and make them a witness to your thoughts.

Try a ploy.
You know the sorts of things you find yourself saying about your neighbours. So treat yourself to your own bad opinion of yourself. You'll soon get used to both telling and hearing the truth.

Basics

- ❖ From every idea or event, even if it first appears far from what you believe, try to discover something that helps your thinking and serves your life.
- ❖ The great people surrender themselves to the inevitable. Only the poor of heart would rather reform nature than themselves.
- ❖ You needn't always walk with the same tread and at the same pace; but you should follow the same path.
- ❖ Don't send your desires on a wild and distant safari. Let them explore what is near to hand.

❖ There are things that are more feasible to eradicate entirely from your life than to regulate. Abstinence is usually easier than moderation.

❖ Learning helpful practices means unlearning unhelpful ones.

❖ Abandon what you know to be impossible, but work hard towards the possible.

❖ We should always try to attain perfection. But at the least we should mould our lives into a compromise between an ideal and the prevailing morality.

❖ All the essential truths should be frequently discussed and borne in mind. Why? So that we not only know them thoroughly but have them always ready to hand.

Remember to set limits: In this way chance won't do it for you.

❖ Examine both yourself and the thing you wish to do. If you find a discrepancy of strength, and believe that you will not succeed, stop there. For the unaccomplished task will defeat you and make you bitter.

❖ And this is an exercise: Apply to your woes the medicines that are cheaply available: learn to practise moderation, rein in extravagance, mitigate ambition and soothe anger.

But be able to see opportunities...

Always consider all the options. If everything in front of you seems closed, look behind you. You'll never find an area closed to you without an even larger one left open.

To reshape events is what's needed.

❖ Be flexible. Don't discover you've put all your energy into one monolithic plan. Follow the path that's offered when it suits your needs.
❖ Take from events, whether good or bad, all they can offer.
❖ To find change disturbing is foreign to feeling calm; for all of life is change.

When you're in trouble, stay with what you believe and withdraw to your own company for a while.

❖ Think your way through problems. Harsh situations can be soothed, boundaries expanded and heaviness lightened if you learn how to bear your difficulties.
❖ Habit can be an ally. We become accustomed to our troubles. Nature invented habit to alleviate them.

Be a friend to yourself and you'll encourage the gods to be kind.

❖ You can't wish anyone worse than to wish them on bad terms with themselves. Even if they appear happy, they're headed for ruin.

About variety
It's always necessary. Alternate solitude with companionship. The first will make you long for a party; the second will make you content to be on your own.

Work: a Short Story

Assess yourself as honestly as you can: construct a true picture of your strengths and weaknesses. We usually over-estimate our capabilities. For example, one person puts great store by his charm and powers of persuasion; another makes too many demands on his money; another finds his body is weaker than he thought it. Brash people often go for jobs requiring tact, while timid souls run for public office. Anti-authoritarian people are continually at loggerheads in hierarchical workplaces. Other people don't realise they haven't the stomach for politics and lack the hypocrisy for it as well; some think themselves delicate but appear bold; still others believe themselves cleverer than they are and indulge in sarcasm, which does them no good at all.

The how of work

- ❖ Decide whether your nature is better suited to practical things or to quiet study and reflection; whether to working alone or in a group. Always take the path created by your disposition: compulsion is not your ally.
- ❖ After assessing yourself, turn to an evaluation of your staying-power. The performer must be stronger than the task.
- ❖ Begin only those things that you can finish in good time. Avoid tasks that become larger as you go along and don't stop where you had intended.

❖ Balance work with rest. Too much work makes you incapable of more. Find your own way in this: either pursue long periods of work followed by relatively lengthy periods of leisure or divide each day into periods of work and rest.
❖ Let your work not be futile, nor the result unworthy of the labour.

And all work and no play…

❖ Non-stop mental labour induces mental dullness and apathy.
❖ Give your mind the gift of relaxation. You'll find it sharper and steadier after a rest. Just as a crop can't be forced, so continuous work will sap the mind's energy.

Reasons to Be Correctly Cheerful: a Few Words on a Big Feeling

Although I'm suggesting that you resist the gifts of luck and avoid those sweet stirrings of hope, I do not wish that you should dispense with joy. On the contrary, you must never be deprived of it.

And do not worry: once you have felt it, it will always be there inside you.

❖ Find joy in yourself and what is best in you.
❖ If you see things as they really are, you'll know that problems more often turn out well than badly for us.
❖ In everyone's life, they will discover things that amuse and relax and please them if they are willing to

bear their troubles lightly rather than make them oppressors.

❖ Like the kindest parents, the gods pile their benefits even on those who doubt them.

❖ Peace of mind consists largely in doing no wrong.

❖ Our goal is to live in tune with nature. It is totally against nature to torture our bodies, to reject basic standards of hygiene or to adopt a tasteless or even disgusting diet. Just as a craving for rich and elaborate food is a sign of extravagance, so the rejection of healthy and tasty food is a warning of insanity. My idea of the good life calls for simple living – not for doing penance.

❖ You don't need to be hard on yourself, telling yourself stop! here, getting angry with yourself there, always pushing yourself through gritted teeth. No, what we need is quiet confidence in ourselves and the belief that we haven't been misled by the people around us. What we need most of all is to be unshaken.

❖ No state is so bitter that a calm mind can't find in it some form of consolation.

Look for the Good before You Sniff out the Bad: a Story

We'd been made happy by examples of courageous and generous and kind acts, and admired them as if they were absolutely perfect. Underneath were flaws, but we blanked these out. For it's natural to make the most of things that deserve our praise and only a crazy person wouldn't yield in favour of the good.

A joke is always useful.

Seneca wrote this:

❖ Whenever I want to be cheered up by an idiot, I don't have far to look. I can laugh at myself.

❖ Instead of loathing destroyers, fools, and oppressors, you'd be better off finding them ridiculous.

One philosopher used to weep when he appeared in public. Another would laugh. To one, all human behaviour seemed abominations; to the other, follies.

And we too should adopt a lighter and more indulgent attitude to life. It is more human to laugh at it than to curse it with lamentations.

And even…

I have nothing against alcohol, particularly wine. Very occasionally you may even get a little drunk – I mean a *little* drunk – for it is helpful in cheering you up, in opening up your mind and in healing grief and in encouraging health. At times we all need a bit of help in enjoying ourselves.

There's Light at the End of the Tunnel

The boat trip to Naples had been such a nightmare that I opted to return by land. Unfortunately, land travel necessitated descent into the Naples tunnel. This must be the world's longest dungeon, with lighting designed to terrify rather than illuminate. Imagine being in a windowless, virtually lightless, seemingly endless hole, soaking up mud and dust through every pore. By the end of it I looked like a very strange sort of cake: coated in mud and then powdered with dust.

Yet that glimpse of one of fate's more ingenious punishments made me think. I felt very adrift and upset. This wasn't due to fear but to a change in my consciousness, a natural reaction I could do nothing about.

The instant I saw the light at the end of the tunnel my normal cheerfulness returned spontaneously. And I thought of how the soul can't be trapped or contained within the body, but will always escape into the air. Which inevitably begs the question: is the soul immortal? I concluded that if it could survive the body, it couldn't be destroyed, and that once in the air, it was eternal.

A Kind of Prayer

Can you prevent me from asking questions? Can't I try to discover how the universe began, and who gave things form? Can I not wonder at the artist who created the world and its abundance, fashioning law and order as well as the light that is perhaps fire or something brighter than fire? Can I not ask? Am I not to know where I'm descended from and whether I shall be on this world only once or be born and born again, or where I am to go when I leave? I was made for too great a destiny to be merely the baggage of my body, which is only a thin chain placed around my freedom. My flesh shall never make me afraid. Even now the soul has supremacy.

VICTORIA RADIN
LONDON, APRIL 2001